NEW ENGLAND REMEMBERS

The Boston Massacre

Robert J. Allison

Robert J. Allison, Series Editor

Commonwealth Editions
Beverly, Massachusetts

For my aunt, Jean Davies,
Who gives us a happier reason to remember the Fifth of March

ISBN-13: 978-1-933212-10-4
ISBN-10: 1-933212-10-1

Library of Congress Cataloging-in-Publication Data
Allison, Robert J.
 The Boston Massacre / Robert J. Allison.
  p. cm. — (New England remembers)
 Includes bibliographical references and index.
 ISBN-13: 978-1-933212-10-4
 ISBN-10: 1-933212-10-1 (alk. paper)
 1. Boston Massacre, 1770. I. Title. II. Series.
 E215.4.A45 2006
 973.3'113—dc22   2006011327

Cover and interior design by Laura McFadden Design, Inc.
laura.mcfadden@rcn.com

Printed in the United States of America.

Commonwealth Editions
266 Cabot Street, Beverly, Massachusetts 01915
www.commonwealtheditions.com

Front cover: 1856 lithograph of the Boston Massacre, courtesy of The Bostonian Society.
Back cover: Boston Massacre monument on Boston Common, courtesy of The Bostonian Society.

The *New England Remembers* series, Robert J. Allison, Series Editor
The Big Dig by James A. Aloisi, Jr.
Boston's Abolitionists by Kerri Greenidge
The Boston Strangler by Alan Rogers
The Cocoanut Grove Fire by Stephanie Schorow
The Hurricane of 1938 by Aram Goudsouzian
Lizzie Borden by Karen Elizabeth Chaney
Sacco & Vanzetti by Eli C. Bortman

The "New England Remembers" logo features a photo of the Thomas Pickton House, Beverly, Massachusetts, used courtesy of the Beverly Historical Society.

CONTENTS

FOREWORD

MONDAY, MARCH 5, 1770. A weekend of tension between British soldiers and Boston rope workers exploded in a riot at Dock Square, which spilled over into King Street. Under attack by the mob, seven British soldiers fired into the crowd. Three men, Crispus Attucks, Samuel Gray, and James Caldwell died on the street; Samuel Maverick and Patrick Carr were dead within the week. The official British report called it an "unhappy disturbance," but Boston leaders immediately called it the "horrid massacre."

Boston's leaders determined that the memory of March 5 would live on. According to Samuel Adams, the event was not a riot, but the inevitable consequence of armed soldiers keeping order in a community that preferred to police itself. One contemporary image of the scene called the shooting the "fruits of arbitrary power," and for Boston leaders the only remedy was to remove not only the troops but also the power of the British government from Boston. The event of March 5, and its annual commemoration, made the American Revolution inevitable.

The British soldiers were later acquitted, defended by John Adams, who denounced the mob that provoked them. Whether the event of March 5 was a riot against British soldiers, or an attack by British power against American liberty, New England remembers the Boston Massacre.

Robert J. Allison, Series Editor
Boston, Massachusetts

CHRONOLOGY

1767
5 NOVEMBER
Customs Commissioners arrive in Boston; Parliament passes Townsend Duties, taxing goods sold in colonies.

1768
OCTOBER
14th and 29th Regiments arrive in Boston.

1770
22 FEBRUARY
Mob of boys attacks Theophilus Lillie's shop; Ebenezer Richardson kills Christopher Seider.

26 FEBRUARY
Funeral of Christopher Seider

5 MARCH
Boston Massacre

6 MARCH
Town meeting at Faneuil Hall has to adjourn to Old South to accommodate overflow crowd; Lt. Gov. Hutchinson calls meeting of Council to discuss episode.

8 MARCH
Funeral of Attucks, Caldwell, Gray, and Maverick; Roxbury town meeting calls for removal of troops from Boston.

10 MARCH
29th Regiment leaves for Castle Island.

11 MARCH
14th Regiment leaves for Castle Island.

12 MARCH
Boston appoints James Bowdoin, Joseph Warren, and Samuel Adams to committee to write account of events of March 5; city considers building monument to victims.

13 MARCH
Town engages Robert Treat Paine to assist with prosecution.

14 MARCH
Patrick Carr dies of his wounds.

15 MARCH
General Court opens meeting at Cambridge, though House of
Representatives protests meeting anywhere but Boston.

16 MARCH
Customs agent John Robinson sails for England, with Dalrymple's
account of events of March 5.

17 MARCH
Patrick Carr buried with other victims in Granary Burying Ground.

19 MARCH
Boston adopts the report "Short Narrative of the Horrid Massacre in
Boston," resolves to have regular orations to commemorate the "bar-
barous murder" and frustrate "conspirators against the public Liberty."
Ebenezer Richardson arraigned for murder of Christopher Seider.

21 APRIL
Ebenezer Richardson found guilty of murdering Christopher Seider

7 SEPTEMBER
Captain Preston, Corporal Wemms, seven soldiers, and four civilians
arraigned for murder of Crispus Attucks and others on March 5.
All plead not guilty.

24 OCTOBER
Preston's trial opens in Superior Court.

30 OCTOBER
Jury acquits Preston.

27 NOVEMBER
Trial of Corporal Wemms and seven soldiers opens.

5 DECEMBER
Jury acquits all but Kilroy and Montgomery, who are found guilty
of manslaughter.

6 DECEMBER
Captain Preston leaves for England.

12 DECEMBER
Four civilians tried for role in Massacre; jury acquits all without leaving their seats.

14 DECEMBER
Kilroy and Montgomery plead benefit of clergy, are branded on hands.

1771
5 MARCH
Dr. Thomas Young delivers memorial address at Manufactory House; church bells toll for an hour; Paul Revere illuminates windows with scenes of Christopher Seider and victims of massacre.

19 MARCH
Boston proposes an annual memorial oration.

28 MARCH
Bourgatte put in pillory as punishment for perjury.

2 APRIL
James Lovell delivers first annual oration at Faneuil Hall; when crowd is too large, it moves to Old South Meeting House.

1772
5 MARCH
Dr. Benjamin Church delivers annual oration at Old South.

10 MARCH
Ebenezer Richardson flees from Boston.

1773
5 MARCH
Dr. Joseph Warren delivers annual oration at Old South; John Adams is invited to speak, but declines.

1774
5 MARCH
John Hancock delivers annual oration at Old South.

1775
5 MARCH
Dr. Joseph Warren delivers annual oration at Old South.

1776
5 MARCH
With British occupying Boston, annual memorial observance at Watertown; Peter Thacher delivers oration.

17 MARCH
British evacuate Boston.

1777
5 MARCH
Benjamin Hichborn delivers annual oration at Old Brick
Meeting House.

1778
5 MARCH
Jonathan Williams Austin, formerly John Adams's law clerk and a
prosecution witness at trial, delivers annual oration at Old Brick
Meeting House.

1779
5 MARCH
Colonel William Tudor delivers annual oration at Old Brick
Meeting House.

1780
5 MARCH
Jonathan Mason delivers annual oration at Old Brick Meeting
House. Christopher Monk dies of wounds sustained.

1781
5 MARCH
Thomas Dawes delivers annual oration at Old Brick Meeting House.

1782
5 MARCH
George Richards Minot delivers oration at Old Brick Meeting
House.

1783
5 MARCH
Dr. Thomas Welsh delivers annual oration at Old Brick. At annual
town meeting at Faneuil Hall, town votes to substitute July 4
celebration for March 5 commemoration.

1840
JUNE
Iron fence built around Granary Burying Ground; excavation
unearths victims of Massacre, who are reintered.

1851

22 FEBRUARY

Seven black Bostonians petition legislature to build monument to Crispus Attucks.

1858

5 MARCH

Boston's black and abolitionist communities observe "Crispus Attucks Day" with rally at Faneuil Hall, protesting Dred Scott decision.

1860

5 MARCH

At Crispus Attucks Day observation in Boston, orator John S. Rock compares John Brown to Crispus Attucks.

1886

Bostonian Society places marker on site of Boston Massacre. Historian John Fiske delivers oration on March 5.

1888

City and state build monument to Boston Massacre on Boston Common and dedicate marker near site of victim's graves.

1900

Crispus Attucks Elementary School founded, Kansas City, Missouri.

1904

Attucks Music Publishing Company, owned and operated by African Americans, founded in New York (becomes Attucks-Gotham in 1905; sold in 1911).

1906

Sons of the American Revolution place marker on grave site of Christopher Seider and Attucks, Gray, Maverick, Caldwell, and Carr.

1916

Attucks High School, in Hopkinsville, Kentucky, a new segregated school for blacks, opens after black protests school committee approval of new white high school.

1919

African Americans in Norfolk, Virginia, build and operate Crispus Attucks Theatre (now the Crispus Attucks Cultural Center) designed by black architect Harvey Johnson.

1931

Crispus Attucks Association formed in York, Pennsylvania, to improve quality of life for African Americans and others.

1932
Massachusetts legislature calls on governor to issue annual proclamation commemorating Boston Massacre.

1955
Coach Ray Crowe and player Oscar Robertson leads the Crispus Attucks High School Tigers basketball team in Indianapolis to the Indiana State Championship.

1976
Boston Equal Rights League dedicates Crispus Attucks memorial in Old State House.

1978
Crispus Attucks Park of the Arts opens on former site of telephone switching station in Washington, D.C.

1981
Massachusetts Council of Minutemen and Militia begins annual re-enactments of Massacre outside Old State House.

1995
Punk-rock band "Crispus Attucks" formed

1998
To support building of Black Patriots Memorial on The Mall in Washington, U.S. Mint issues commemorative coin featuring Crispus Attucks.

1999
At opening of new Suffolk Law School on site of Manufactory House in Boston, students, faculty, and alumni re-enact trial of Wemms and British soldiers.

2004
Artist Frano Violich creates art installation *Material Witness* featuring teapot thought to have belonged to Crispus Attucks.

CHAPTER ONE

Building Tensions

IN OCTOBER 1768, TWO REGIMENTS of British troops, the 14th and 29th regiments, arrived in Boston. They came at the request of Royal Governor Francis Bernard who thought the troops would keep order in Boston and also help customs officials collect the taxes Parliament had levied. The Massachusetts Assembly, elected every year by the people of the province, thought that only they, the representatives elected by the people, could levy taxes in Massachusetts. The assembly charged that Bernard was bringing in troops to subvert their government. The town of Boston, governed by a town meeting, believed the troops unnecessary to keep order.

But Bernard had reason to think the troops were essential to enforcing British law. Earlier that year, in June, when customs officials had seized a sloop belonging to merchant and political leader John Hancock, a group called the "Sons of Liberty" had freed the ship. The Sons of Liberty gathered beneath a large elm in Boston's South End (near today's intersection of Washington and Essex streets), decorating this "Liberty Tree" with placards, lanterns, and effigies of officials like Bernard or tax collectors. Bernard saw the Sons of Liberty as a lawless mob; he believed that he needed troops to prevent their lawlessness from overwhelming the legitimate government—indeed, he believed that the troops were essential to keep peace. Others, however, thought the troops would provoke, not prevent, disorder. Benjamin Franklin, a

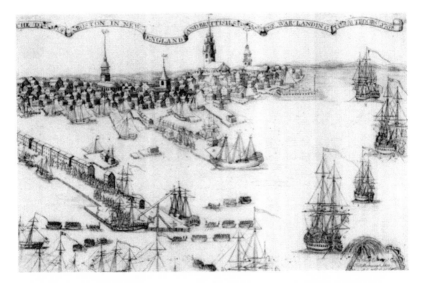

Paul Revere engraved this scene of the British troops landing at Boston in 1768. He emphasized Boston's church steeples, implying that Bostonians were religious people who did not need troops to keep order. (Courtesy of the Massachusetts Archives)

native Bostonian now living in England, feared what would happen when the "the madness of mobs, or the interference of soldiers, or both, when too near each other, might occasion some mischief difficult to be prevented or repaired, and which might spread far and wide."

Paul Revere, a North End silversmith and a Son of Liberty, made an engraving of the arrival of British forces. The engraving's most prominent features are the church steeples of Boston, suggesting that Bostonians were religious and orderly people who did not need troops to enforce the law.

The troops did not help keep the peace. In fact, their presence made a tense situation worse. Two thousand British soldiers, trying to keep order in a town of sixteen thousand, strained Boston's resources. Bernard wanted the town of Boston to provide lodging for the troops, but the town's government, the leaders of the town meeting held in Faneuil Hall, insisted that the soldiers be kept at Bernard's expense in the fort on Castle Island (now in South Boston), three miles from downtown. After all, town meeting members argued, they had not

John Singleton Copley painted this portrait of silversmith and Son of Liberty Paul Revere in 1768. (Courtesy of the Museum of Fine Arts, Boston)

asked for the soldiers; therefore they were Bernard's responsibility, not Boston's. Not wanting to have his troops so far away as Castle Island, Bernard temporarily quartered some of the troops in Faneuil Hall, where the town meeting met, and then in the Old State House, where the assembly met. This outraged both the town leaders and the assembly and convinced the townspeople that Bernard really meant to subvert their government. Bernard tried to find another town building for his troops and decided on the Manufactory House, a building across from the Granary Burying ground, occupied by poor tenants. The tenants refused to let the soldiers in, however, and the soldiers surrounded the building in hopes of starving them out. But townspeople rallied to the tenants' cause, lobbing loaves of bread and roasts of meat into the Manufactory House's upper windows. After two weeks, the siege of the Manufactory House ended, with Bernard acknowledging that the soldiers had to be housed at his expense. He rented space in several warehouses and wharves for barracks. Some of the soldiers, who had come with their families, rented rooms from townspeople.

The troops were in Boston to help customs inspectors enforce the law. Leaders in the town wanted the troops removed and the customs laws repealed. Samuel Adams, a leader of Boston's town meeting and a representative to the Massachusetts Assembly, organized a boycott of the goods that Parliament had taxed: lead, paint, glass, tea, and other British manufactures. Bostonians had no voice in Parliament, so Adams hoped the boycott would hurt British merchants enough that they would pressure Parliament to rescind the taxes. Only by exerting indirect pressure could Bostonians hope to change British policy. According to Thomas Hutchinson, Governor Bernard's lieutenant governor, however, the boycotts did not "greatly impact the British merchants" and "the Tradesmen & Manufacturers do not feel it."

With the boycott not working, Samuel Adams and the Sons of Liberty did more to enforce it. The British soldiers could not protect merchants who sold British goods when the Sons of Liberty ransacked their shops and then hanged the merchants in effigy on the Liberty Tree. Governor Bernard left for England, determined to call for more British force in Boston, as the Sons of Liberty stepped up their campaign of intimidation in 1769. When the pro-Parliamentary *Boston Chronicle* criticized the boycott in October 1769, the Sons of Liberty attacked its office and destroyed its printing press.

In February 1770, news reached Boston that British troops in New York had cut down the "Liberty Pole" there, but the Sons of Liberty in that city had resisted effectively. Not to be outdone by the New Yorkers, Boston's Sons of Liberty knew they needed to take more action. They began putting up signs identifying boycott-violating merchants. Each sign was in the form of a large pointing hand, bearing the word "IMPORTER." Once a sign was posted, crowds of schoolboys would gather outside the shop, taunting anyone who dared to go inside and pelting them with horse dung when they came out. On February 22, a sign went up outside the North End shop of Theophilus Lillie, and the usual crowd gathered to harass away any buyers. When Lillie's neighbor Ebenezer Richardson—already notorious among the Sons of Liberty for his work as an informer (he had alerted customs officials that Hancock's sloop was carrying unreported goods)—tried to tear down the sign, the crowd of boys turned on him, pelting him with sticks and dirt, driving him back to his own house. Richardson spied one of the leading Sons of Liberty and some other men standing on the other side of the street. He shouted, "Perjury! Perjury!" and "By the eternal God I'll make it too hot for you before night."

As Richardson locked his door behind him, Son of Liberty Thomas Knox shouted, "Come out, you damn son of a bitch! I'll have your heart out, your liver out!" Richardson did come out, shaking his fists at the crowd of boys and the men who egged them on, telling the boys to get out of the street. Stones rained down on him, breaking his front window, breaking the door. His wife and daughters were hit with stones through the broken panes. George Wilmot, a sailor, came to Richardson's aid, and the two of them found guns. Boys now were in Richardson's backyard, attacking from the rear. Now Richardson and Wilmot appeared at the front window with muskets. Richardson threatened that if they did not leave "he'd make it too hot for 'em, as sure as there was a God in heaven, he'd blow a Lane through 'em" with his gun. He knelt, resting his gun on the windowsill, and fired.

The pellets from Richardson's gun tore through sailor Robert Patterson's pants, wounded another young man's right hand, and pierced the chest and abdomen of eleven-year-old Christopher Seider, who was just bending down to pick up another rock.

Seider was carried off, badly wounded but still alive. No one knew who he was, his name was spelled Seider or Snyder. But now that he

Paul Revere crafted this bowl to honor the Sons of Liberty in 1768. To this day, Boston's mayors present replicas of this bowl to visiting dignitaries. (Courtesy of the Museum of Fine Arts, Boston)

was dying, they stormed the house. Richardson and Wilmot would both have been lynched had radical leader William Molineux not intervened. As the judge Peter Oliver noted, Molineux and the other radicals "were pretty sure that they could procure a Jury for Conviction," so they wanted Richardson "hanged by the forms of Law, rather than suffer the Disgrace of Hangmen themselves." Through the streets to the jail the crowd dragged Wilmot and Richardson.

At nine that night Christopher Seider died. Samuel Adams arranged for his funeral, at town expense, to be held at Faneuil Hall, the town's official public gathering place, on Monday, February 26. Two thousand people followed Seider's casket, carried by six youths, as his body was taken from Faneuil Hall, down and around the Liberty Tree and back to the Old State House, then to the Granary Burying Ground. "My eyes never beheld such a funeral," John Adams wrote. "The Ardor of the People is not to be quelled by the Slaughter of one Child and the Wounding of Another." Spelling his name "Snider," the poet Phillis Wheatley wrote of the funeral:

> Snider behold with what Majestic Love
> The Illustrious retinue begins to move
> With secret rage fair freedom's foes beneath
> See in thy corse ev'n Majesty in Death.

THERE MAY HAVE BEEN MAJESTY in Seider's death, but the incident and the funeral exposed a nerve, a tension between the Sons of Liberty and the importing merchants, and a continuing disdain for the British soldiers brought to town to enforce the customs laws. On Friday, March 2, Patrick Walker, a soldier from the 29th Regiment, was walking past John Gray's South End ropewalk, a long building where men stretched and twisted strands of hemp into rope. Knowing that the poorly paid British soldiers were always looking for part-time jobs (in fact, the British soldiers competed with the poorer Bostonians for menial work), one of men called out, "Do you want work?"

"Yes," Walker said, "I do, by faith."

"Well, go clean my shit house."

"By God," Walker shouted at this insult, "I'll have satisfaction!" He swung a punch at rope worker Nicholas Ferriter, who knocked Walker off his feet. As Walker fell, his coat flew open and his cutlass fell out. Ferriter walked off with the soldier's sword, while Walker got up and stormed away.

Twenty minutes later, Walker was back with ten or twelve soldiers, including Private William Warren, ready to take up the argument. Why had the workers "abused" Walker, they asked? The rope workers, agitated, sent word down the walk "for the hands to come up," and after "several knocks amongst" them, they drove the soldiers away. About three-quarters of an hour later, thirty soldiers, this time with Private Matthew Kilroy and a "tall Negro drummer with a cutlass chained to his body," were back to fight. An elderly neighbor, John Hill, saw the group approaching and called to the drummer, "You black rascal, what have you to do with white people's quarrels?"

"I suppose I may look on," the drummer said as the soldiers stormed into the ropewalk. Again the rope workers drove them out, this time all the way back to their barracks, where a corporal ordered the soldiers back inside.

The next afternoon, Archibald McNeil was at work with two apprentices at his own ropewalk when three soldiers came in, demanding, "You damn dogs, don't you deserve to be killed?" None of the workers replied, but when provoked, one of the apprentices said, "Damn it, I know what a grenadier is." One of the soldiers took a swing at him, and the workers drove the soldiers away with clubs.

That evening, a Saturday, John Gray heard that soldiers from the 29th Regiment were going to attack his men on Monday morning, March 5. He resolved to go speak to Colonel William Dalrymple, commander of the 14th Regiment and the senior army officer in Boston on Monday, but at about noon on Sunday he learned that Lieutenant Colonel Maurice Carr of the 29th Regiment had ordered a search of Gray's ropewalk, suspecting that a missing sergeant may have been murdered there. Gray was furious that his ropewalks had been searched without his consent, and he did not wait but complained to Dalrymple immediately. He told Dalrymple what he had heard of the fight on Friday; Dalrymple said he had heard much the same story. Agreeing that his employee had provoked the fight, Gray resolved to fire him the next day. He would do all he could to "prevent my people's giving them any affront in the future," and Dalrymple pledged to keep his men in their barracks.

As Dalrymple and Gray were resolving this problem, Colonel Carr came in. Once again the rope workers were beating up his soldiers, he said, and further he was "searching for a sergeant who had been murdered."

Gray asked why Carr thought the sergeant would be in his rope-walk. If he had come directly to Gray, instead of breaking into the rope-walk, Gray "would have waited on him, and opened every apartment I had for his satisfaction."

In the meantime, rumors swirled through town that there would be trouble. A rope worker told his landlord, Benjamin Burdick, that soldiers were following him. Burdick armed himself with his Highland broadsword for protection and would not hesitate to use it. When he saw a soldier outside his house (who told Burdick he was "pumping ship," that is, urinating), he "beat him till he had enough of it," and the soldier fled.

On Monday morning, March 5, a handbill was posted throughout the streets of Boston:

> *this is to inform ye Rebellious People in Boston, that ye Soldiers in ye 14th and 29th Regiments are determend to Joine together and Defend themselves against all who Shall Oppose them.*
> *Signed ye Soldiers of ye 14th and 29th Regiments*

Who wrote the handbill? Who posted it? Probably not the soldiers, but someone determined to increase the trouble between the soldiers and the rope workers. Governor Bernard had thought the troops were essential to enforce the law; Samuel Adams and the Sons of Liberty believed the presence of the troops violated the law. But the question was no longer abstract: the soldiers and townspeople had begun to fight. Would men like John Gray and Colonel Dalrymple be able to keep peace, or would violence continue?

CHAPTER TWO

The Fatal Fifth of March

ON MONDAY EVENING, March 5, 1770, crowds of men and boys armed with shovels, sticks, and swords began converging on Dock Square, in front of Faneuil Hall, about eight o'clock. Half a dozen unarmed teenagers broke into the market on lower floors of Faneuil Hall and broke apart the butchers' stalls for wood. Sergeant Major William Davies of the 14th Regiment wisely changed into civilian clothes after hearing the youths promise to "murder the first Officer or Soldier they should meet with." Bostonian Archibald Gould was afraid to go home because he saw so many people "walking from all Quarters with sticks," not ordinary canes but "Cudgells" and branches of hedge. The people carrying them were "in such Commotion as I hardly ever saw in my life."

Rumors—that a soldier in Dock Square had hurt an oysterman, that the soldiers were going to cut down the Liberty Tree—brought more people. By eight-thirty, two to three hundred armed and angry people were in Dock Square. A mysterious man in a red cloak and white wig focused the crowd's attention and "harangued them about three minutes," and then the impassioned crowd "huzza'd" for the Main Guard, storming off to attack the main barracks across from the Old State House. Up Corn Hill (now the southwestern part of City Hall Plaza) went one contingent, headed for Murray's Barracks, where the 29th Regiment was housed. Others marched down Exchange Lane toward the Main Guard.

Murray's Barracks was a sugar warehouse, which has since been replaced by the brick expanse of City Hall Plaza. The only approach to the barracks was through a gate and a narrow passageway. Soldiers armed with shovels, clubs, bayonets, or cutlasses were able to hold their ground and fend off the attack. Seven or eight soldiers chased part of the crowd down through Boylston's Alley (which still runs from City Hall Plaza to Court Street), but this only infuriated the rest, particularly when a young boy, six or seven years old, came back through the crowd with his face bleeding.

When merchant Benjamin Davis saw the crowd pressing at the entrance to Boylston's Alley, he heard that "it was the town's people and soldiers a quarreling," though to him it sounded more "like people fighting with clubs." Two young men asked Davis if he was going help fight soldiers, then they ran into the alley shouting, "Fire! Fire!" to raise the general alarm with townspeople. Davis stepped out of the way as nine or ten soldiers ran up the alley carrying clubs and other weapons.

"Town-born, turn out!" a man cried, repeating the call twenty or thirty times. "Fire!" and "Town-born, turn out!" were both emergency calls—for a fire, all would turn out of their homes to put out the fire, which could destroy the entire town; the "town-born" were particularly responsible to protect their community. "Who is that man?" shouted Ensign Alexander Mall of the 29th to the sentinel. "Lay hold of him."

But the sentinel could not stop him. Other townspeople had gotten into the Old Brick Meeting House just west of the Old State House to ring the bell, a signal for fire that would bring more men into the streets. The crowd continued to push at the gates to the barracks but could not break through. The officers kept their soldiers inside the gates, but the crowd now fired snowballs over onto the soldiers. One soldier took his musket, and kneeling down before Boylston's Alley said, "God Damn your blood I'le make a Lane through you all." Ensign Mall and two others grabbed hold of him and dragged him back into the barracks. Seeing the disorder, Captain John Goldfinch of the 14th Regiment came through the crowd, calling through the gates that the soldiers were to return to the barracks. Goldfinch joined the officers of the 29th Regiment on the steps of the barracks and urged them to bring the men inside before they had a riot on their hands.

"Why don't you keep your soldiers in the barracks?" Son of Liberty Richard Palmes called to the officers. The officers shouted that they were keeping them in the barracks. "Are the inhabitants to be knocked down in the streets and murdered in this manner?" Palmes shouted back. The officers repeated that they were keeping their men in the barracks. "We did not send for you," another man shouted. "We won't have you here. We'll get rid of you, we'll drive you away!"

"Home! Home!" the crowd began to chant. Snowballs began to hit the barracks door behind the officers. An officer asked Palmes, who seemed to have some authority, to disperse the crowd. The officer promised that no soldiers would come out. "You mean they dare not come out," someone shouted. "Damn the soldiers," they were "a Pack of Scoundrells they dared not come out and fight them," the disappointed men said as they moved away from the barracks and down toward King Street. "We shall find some soldiers in King Street," some were saying. Some wanted to attack the Main Guard, stationed just across from the Old State House; others stopped in front of the Brazen Head, a King Street tavern owned by importer William Jackson's mother. Captain Thomas Preston of the 29th also lodged at the Brazen Head.

"Damn it, here lives an importer," someone said as the crowd began to hit the windows; others picked up chunks of ice to smash the glass. After a neighbor warned them not to break the windows, the crowd moved on down King Street.

Captain John Goldfinch had left the 29th's barracks to return to his own regiment. As he passed through King Street, barber's apprentice Edward Gerrish accused him of not paying his barber's bill. Goldfinch, who had the receipt in his pocket, thought the boy's taunt was "a premeditated Plan, and designed as an affront to the military in Gen'ral," because in Boston at this time, "any Man that wore the King's Commission was liable to be insulted any Hour of the Night." As Goldfinch moved on, Gerrish turned to Hugh White, the lone British sentry standing guard in front of the Custom House, down King Street from the Old State House. As Gerrish and a dozen other apprentices moved in on him, White used his musket to push them back.

White soon found himself surrounded. "There's the son of a bitch that knocked me down," an apprentice called out, and the others closed in. "Kill him, kill him, knock him down." Town constable Edward

Langford told them to leave the sentry alone and told White "not to be afraid, they are only boys, and would not hurt him." Though they "were swearing and speaking bad words," Langford recalled later, they were not throwing anything. White retreated from his sentry box to the safer ground of the Custom House steps.

Nineteen-year-old bookseller Henry Knox saw White load his musket and then wave it at the fifteen or twenty youths surrounding him "in the position that they call charged bayonets." He told White that "if he fired he must die for it." According to one account, White retorted, "Damn them, if they molest me, I will fire." The youths taunted White: "Fire and be damned!" Knox pushed one of the apprentices aside, and another youth said, "God damn him, we will knock him down for snapping." Sailor James Bailey, who had been in Saturday's fight at the ropewalks, saw pieces of ice "as big as your fist" being hurled at White, who told Bailey he didn't know what had brought the attack on, but "if the Boys did not disperse, there would be something by and by."

Now the Brattle Street Church bell in Brattle Square (roughly now the site of the Government Center T entrance) was ringing. Hearing the bells, more people poured into the streets, looking for a fire. Newton Prince, a free black pastry cook, came out to fight the fire. He learned "there was no fire but there was going to be something better, a fight."

From his North End boardinghouse, Patrick Keaton came out to Union Street when he heard the alarm. Following the crowd to Dock Square, he learned that a boy and a soldier had been in a fight. Along came Crispus Attucks, a tall, strong sailor and runaway slave, leading twenty-five or thirty men up Corn Hill. Attucks was carrying "two clubs in his hand" and offered one to Keaton. Keaton joined Attucks's group but dropped the club in the snow.

Attucks and his contingent joined the crowd, now fifty or sixty strong, pressing around Hugh White, the sentinel, and more were gathered across King Street. Trying to get help, White struck the brass knocker on the Custom House door, but there was no response. Two young men raced to tell the officers up the street at the Main Guard house, across from the Old State House, "You must send help to the sentry for I heard 'em say they would kill the sentinel." William Jackson (an importer and British sympathizer) rushed to his mother's tavern, where Captain Preston lodged. Preston hurried back to the barracks, and now he summoned a rescue party for White: Corporal William Wemms and six privates. Preston had the men form two lines and march down King Street.

Wemms led the soldiers through the crowd, using their bayonets to open a path to the Custom House. Snowballs, ice, and oyster shells rained down on the soldiers and the walls of the Custom House as the crowd taunted the soldiers with cheers, curses, and insults. The crowd knew the soldiers were legally forbidden to fire unless a civil magistrate—a judge or a justitce of the peace—read the Riot Act, which made it a "felony for twelve rioters to continue together for an hour after the reading of a proclamation . . . to disperse." If the crowd did not disperse within an hour of the reading of the Riot Act, then and only then could the soldiers fire. Knowing this—and knowing that the soldiers knew it—the crowd continued to taunt, threaten, and throw ice and oyster shells at the soldiers.

When James Murray, justice of the peace and owner of Murray's Barracks, was spotted on the outskirts of King Street, witnesses "heard the people halloo here comes Murray with the Riot Act," and then the crowd turned to pelt someone who ran down Pudding Lane.

In front of the Custom House, young colonial Henry Knox took hold of Captain Preston's coat, warning, "For God's sake take care of your Men for if they fire your life must be answerable."

"I am sensible of it," an agitated Preston replied.

Preston had had a simple plan: to have sentry Hugh White join the line of soldiers and thus to bring him safely back to the barracks. Now, however, they were trapped in front of the Custom House. One of the privates brandished his bayonet at the sailor James Bailey, but White told him to leave Bailey—who earlier had tried to intercede on White's behalf—alone.

Now there were few voices of moderation in the crowd. A witness recalled that the "people called out fire, damn you why don't you fire, you can't kill us." Standing next to Preston, a colonial began taunting him: "Fire! Why don't you fire!" Richard Palmes stepped between the two men and put his left hand gently on Preston's shoulder. "Are your soldiers' guns loaded?" he asked.

"With powder and ball."

"Sir, I hope you don't intend the Soldiers shall fire on the Inhabitants?"

"By no means," Preston said.

Benjamin Burdick, armed with a club and his broadsword, asked Private Hugh Montgomery, standing at Preston's right, if the soldiers were loaded.

"Yes," Montgomery answered. Would they fire? Burdick asked.

"Yes, by the eternal God," said Montgomery, as he pushed Burdick back with his bayonet. Using his broadsword to push away the bayonet, Burdick hit Montgomery's gunlock.

At this very instant a piece of wood thrown from Exchange Lane came down and hit Montgomery, who staggered. Crispus Attucks now grabbed for his bayonet. Recovering his footing, Montgomery raised his gun and fired. At the same instant another soldier fired.

Two balls tore into Attucks's chest, goring his lungs and liver. Another took off part of Samuel Gray's head. Their two bodies fell to the street.

"Why did you fire?" Preston roared at his men. Hearing only the final word in the midst of the mayhem, the British soldiers thought Preston had given the order to fire. Three more muskets fired. Sailor James Caldwell was making his way across King Street when a shot tore through his back. He died where he lay.

Now Palmes knocked Montgomery's gun from his hands, then turned and tried to hit Preston, but he slipped on the ice and he fell to the ground. The soldiers began to reload. Some in the crowd gave three cheers and others said, "Let's go in upon them, and prevent their firing again." But the soldiers fired as the crowd began its assault. Robert Patterson was putting on his hat to join the charge when a musket ball went through his right arm. Two apprentices, Christopher Monk and John Clark, were hit. Across King Street, in Quaker Lane, Patrick Carr fell to the ground as a ball tore through his hip. Merchant Edward Payne was standing on his porch across King Street when a musket ball shattered his arm. Shouting "Murder" after the first round, apprentice Samuel Maverick retreated up King Street toward the Old State House. A ball from the second round ricocheted off a building and hit him in the chest, cutting through his liver and lodging in his lower ribs. He made it home to his mother, where he died the next morning. Musket balls hit tailor John Green and apprentice David Parker in the legs.

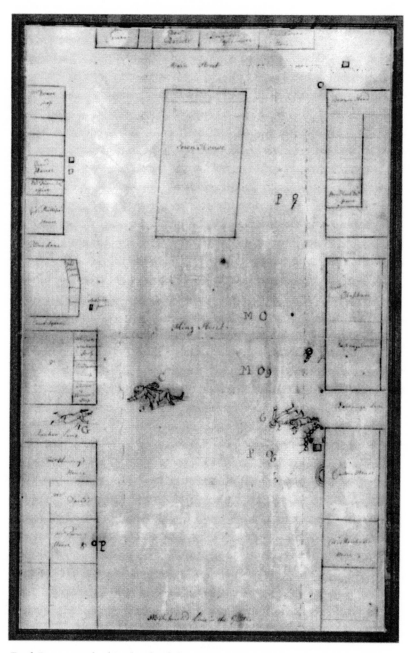

Paul Revere made this sketch of the crime scene within a day or two of the massacre. (Courtesy of the Boston Public Library)

More bells were ringing now, and the noise and rumors brought even more people into King Street. Within a few minutes, more than a thousand people crowded into the area. Even before the soldiers fired, "one upon another came running" to Lieutenant Governor Thomas Hutchinson's North End home (Governor Bernard had left for England in the fall), urging him to come out immediately or else "the whole Town would be in arms and the most bloody scene would follow that had ever been known in America." Hutchinson hurried out to find "vast crowds of People running for their arms." He called them to follow him to King Street, "promising them justice should be done." As he neared the scene, "a great body of men many of them armed with clubs & some with cutlasses, & all calling for the firearms" surrounded him. Unable to get through the angry crowd, he ducked into a private home, and then took the back alleys to King Street.

"The Governor!" cried voices in the crowd as Hutchinson pushed his way toward the line of soldiers in front of the Custom House. As he pressed forward "almost upon the Bayonets," he called for the commanding officer. Preston stepped out from behind the line of soldiers.

"Why did you fire without orders from a civil magistrate?" Hutchinson demanded. He thought Preston seemed "offended at being questioned," and the captain hesitated before he spoke.

"I was obliged to, to save my Sentry."

"You must know it, sir," Hutchinson demanded, meaning that Preston must have been certain that his sentry was in mortal peril.

A bystander remarked loudly. "Then you have murdered three or four men to save your sentry." Others in the crowd began to shout, "To the Town House! To the Town House!" Joseph Belknap, standing beside Hutchinson, urged him to go to the council chamber in the Old State House, if only for his own safety. Hutchinson prevailed on Preston to take his men back to their barracks, as the crowd was growing and the only way to prevent further violence was to get the soldiers off the streets. Preston and his soldiers marched back to the guardhouse, and outside it other men from the 29th Regiment formed a defensive barrier, their weapons aimed at the crowd.

Hutchinson was practically carried by the people up King Street to the Old State House, and once inside he made his way upstairs to the council chamber. Stepping out onto the balcony, where he could sur-

Lieutenant Governor Thomas Hutchinson (1711–1780) detested the Boston mob, but wanted justice done. (Courtesy of the Massachusetts State Art Commission)

vey the whole scene on the street below, Hutchinson called out for the people to go to their homes. A gentleman on the street called up to Hutchinson to order the soldiers to go inside the guardhouse, but Hutchinson said that he could not command the troops. He would send for Colonel Dalrymple. Another man called for Hutchinson to look out the window facing the guardhouse "to see the position the soldiers were in, ready to fire on the inhabitants." Hutchinson did so, and when he saw that indeed the soldiers were aiming at the crowd, he called across the street for the men to be ordered inside. Finally, the soldiers of the 29th shouldered their guns and marched inside.

Hutchinson again called for the crowds to go home. He repeated that he would see that justice was done. The affair was now in the hands of the law, he averred, and "I will live and die by the law."

The crowd began to disperse from King Street; Samuel Gray's friends left his body on Dr. Loring's doorstep. James Caldwell's body was taken to the prison house, and then to the home of his employer; Patrick Carr was carried to a nearby house where a doctor was called, but later he was taken to a private home where he lingered in agony for a week before succumbing; the body of Crispus Attucks, a stranger in town, was taken to the Royal Exchange Tavern, where it was on display the next day, before the town resolved to honor Attucks by having his funeral conducted from Faneuil Hall.

Even with the crowd dispersing, the anger remained. Some townspeople tried to light a signal fire on Beacon Hill to alert other towns of Boston's need for aid, but Hutchinson managed to prevent them from doing so. Still, news of the killings traveled to surrounding towns, which began to mobilize to protect Boston from the British troops. Hutchinson spent the night hearing witnesses in the council chamber, and by dawn it became clear that the soldiers might be criminally responsible. "How far the affronts and abuses offered by the Inhabitants may avail to excuse this Action is uncertain," he wrote to Governor Francis Bernard in England, "but it is certain that nothing more unfortunate could have happened for a very great part of the people are in a perfect frenzy by means of it." In addition to hearing witnesses, Hutchinson summoned the other members of the Governor's Council to an emergency meeting the next morning. By then, Captain Preston had surrendered himself to the authorities, and Corporal Wemms and Privates Hugh Montgomery, James Hartigan, William McCauley, Hugh White (the sentry), John Carroll, William Warren, and Matthew Kilroy were under arrest.

The Horrid Massacre
and Revolutionary Politics

THE NEXT MORNING, the council advised Hutchinson to call in the military officers—Dalrymple and Carr—to shed more light on the problem. He would have liked the commissioners and judge of the Admiralty to be present, too, but he knew the Governor's Council would never allow so much military presence. The council, however, already seemed to know where the solution lay. Several members said that "the people of this and some of the neighboring towns were so exasperated and incensed on account of the inhumane & barbarous destruction of a number of the Inhabitants by the Troops that they apprehended imminent danger of further bloodshed, unless the Troops were forthwith removed from the body of the Town, which in their opinion was the only method to prevent it."

This was an ironic twist. For two weeks, Hutchinson had been calling for the Massachusetts Assembly and Council to move out of Boston, arguing that "tumultuous assemblies of the people" made it a poor place for the government to sit. Now, the morning after the most tumultuous assembly in the province's history, the council itself was calling for the troops to leave. While the council debated the issue, a delegation from the Boston town meeting, convened at Faneuil Hall, arrived to present the town's view of the previous night's events.

Town meeting members had gathered to meet at Faneuil Hall, but when more than three thousand people tried to crowd in, the meeting was moved to the more spacious Old South Meeting House. There the men of the town of Boston had unanimously agreed that the people and the soldiers could no longer peacefully coexist, and that only the removal of the troops would restore order. A delegation led by John Hancock, Samuel Adams, and William Molineux was sent to ask Hutchinson to "use his power and influence . . . for their instant removal."

Hutchinson sent back a message to the town that Colonel Dalrymple could not move the troops without orders from General Thomas Gage, but recognizing that the 29th Regiment was involved in trouble, he would send them to Castle Island. He also would put the 14th Regiment "under such restraint that all future differences may be prevented."

That afternoon a delegation from town meeting informed Hutchinson that both regiments had to go—"nothing will satisfy the Town less than a total and immediate removal of the Troops." The Governor's Council agreed, "aggressively" and "with one voice." Indeed, councilors warned that if Dalrymple did not remove the troops, "the people would most certainly drive out the Troops and . . . the Inhabitants of the Town would join in it." A mob had ransacked his own house in the Stamp Act riots of 1765, and ever since then Hutchinson had resisted any appeasement of the Boston mob. He feared that removal of the troops would allow the mob to attack the customs commissioners. But the council now told him that removing the troops was "the determination not of a mob but of the generality of the . . . Inhabitants." Councilor Royall Tyler told Hutchinson that there were three thousand people meeting now, and "that before next morning 10,000 men would be assembled on the Common of Boston." These were not the kind of people who had destroyed Hutchinson's house; rather, they were "Persons of the first Consequence and Estates in the Country, and men of Religion."

Reluctantly, Hutchinson and the officers agreed to send the troops, along with the customs commissioners, to Castle Island for their own safety.

Although troops had successfully turned away the mob from the 29th Regiment's barracks, the attack on the lone sentry in front of the Custom House had provoked soldiers into firing on the crowd, leaving four dead and one, Patrick Carr, mortally wounded, and seven others

Samuel Adams (1722-1803) led the Boston Town Meeting and organized the official town reponse to the event he would call the "Bloody Massacre." John Singleton Copley painted his portrait in 1773. (Courtesy of the Museum of Fine Arts, Boston)

seriously injured. Would there be more violence? What would happen to the soldiers? Would the customs commissioners be safe in Boston? Lieutenant Governor Hutchinson, heartsick at the violence, was not alone in his belief that the street fight of March 5 might escalate into something more serious.

THOUGH THURSDAY, MARCH 8, was a market day, no shops opened in Boston that day. It would be a day of mourning. Between four and five o'clock in the afternoon, the body of Crispus Attucks was taken from Faneuil Hall. Attucks, who was half African American and half Native American, had no family in town to arrange a funeral, so Samuel Adams did so, holding the service, as he had for Christopher Seider just two weeks earlier, in Faneuil Hall.

Samuel Maverick's mother, Mary, saw her son's casket taken from their house on Union Street, and the young apprentice's mourners followed it toward King Street. James Caldwell's body had been prepared for burial at the home of Captain Morton, and now it joined the others at King Street. From the Exchange Street home of Benjamin Gray

The **Boston Gazette** *showed the caskets of the victims, and turned them into martyrs. (Courtesy of the Bostonian Society)*

came the casket carrying Samuel Gray's body. As the four processions converged on King Street, where the four strangers had been shot, all the church bells in Boston, Roxbury, and Charlestown began to toll.

From the site of the shooting the procession passed up to Main Street (what is today Washington Street) and then wound down toward the Liberty Tree near Boston Neck. Behind the caskets stretched "an immense concourse of people," walking six abreast through the narrow streets, followed by a long train of carriages carrying the "principal Gentry" of Boston. Observers thought more people were gathered this day "than were ever together on this Continent on any Occasion."

After passing the Liberty Tree, the procession moved to the Common and made its way to the Granary Burying Ground. The four caskets were laid together in one grave, next to the body of Christopher Seider. Samuel Adams had orchestrated this public funeral to keep attention focused on the victims, who were buried not as individuals but together, as martyrs.

Four days later, Monday, March 12, town meeting appointed James Bowdoin, Joseph Warren, and Samuel Pemberton to prepare "a particular account" of the "massacre in King Street" so that a "full and just representation" could be made. Between March 13 and March 19, justices of the peace took depositions from ninety-six witnesses. Richard Dana and John Hill, who took most of the depositions, invited Colonel Dalrymple, deputy customs collector William Sheaffe, and Bartholomew Green, whose family lived in the Custom House, to attend and cross-examine witnesses. From these depositions, Bowdoin, Warren, and Pemberton prepared the official town account of the event, which the town meeting accepted on March 19, and ordered copies printed so it could be sent to influential men in England, including member of Parliament Isaac Barre, former governor Thomas Pownall, and Benjamin Franklin, in London representing the Pennsylvania, Georgia, and New Jersey assemblies.

The report, titled *Short Narrative of the Horrid Massacre in Boston, Perpetrated in the Evening of the Fifth Day of March 1770, By Soldiers of the 29th Regiment*, began its narrative of events with the Stamp Act, which had interrupted the "happy union" between Great Britain and its colonies. Harmony had been restored when Parliament repealed the Stamp Act, but then other tax laws, along with the appointment of customs commissioners, had been detrimental "not only to the commerce, but to the political interests of the town and province." From the arrival of the customs commissioners in November 1767, "we can trace . . . the causes of the late horrid massacre." The commissioners had engaged in politics, siding with Governor Francis Bernard "in his political schemes," firing an employee who voted against their interests. The commissioners's inaccessibility and "supercilious behavior" had made them "disgustful to the people in general."

These commissioners, not the soldiers, had precipitated the trouble. The troops were an embarrassment, forced on them by the commissioners' demands, in violation of the Magna Carta and the English Bill of Rights. The troops were a visible symbol of the loss of liberty that had begun when the commissioners arrived. Governor Bernard had seemed to reinforce this idea by quartering the troops in the Old State House, in the very hall where the House of Representatives met, as well as on the lower floor, where the town merchants sold their wares. Although he had removed the troops from the House of Representatives, he moved the Main Guard to a private house "not twelve yards from" the Old State House, and two field guns were aimed at the Old State House. Positioning troops in this way "seemed to indicate an attack upon the constitution, and a defiance of law; and to be intended to affront the legislative and executive authority of the province."

It had become clear that "such conservators of the peace" meant no good. In fact, townspeople now felt the need to arm themselves whenever they ventured into the streets. The *Short Narrative* pointed out that the soldiers had been behaving badly, challenging inhabitants, attacking magistrates, "exciting the negroes of the town to take away their masters' lives and property," firing their muskets in crowded streets. In fact, the brawl at Gray's rope walk had begun when a "soldier challenged the ropemakers to a boxing match."

But though the *Short Narrative* blamed a soldier for starting the fight at the ropewalk and for provoking ordinary people to acts of violence, it argued that the soldiers were mere tools in the hands of the customs commissioners. And it asserted that the soldiers were not the only killers. Five out of ninety-six depositions printed in the *Short Narrative* mentioned seeing a flash coming from the windows of the Custom House.

One other witness reported that he had seen some soldiers go into the Custom House and shut the door before the firing began.

Based on these six depositions, the *Short Narrative* charged that the customs commissioners had themselves fired into the crowd. An anonymous memo in Francis Bernard's papers says that the "whole drift" of the town's inquiry "was to draw in the Custom House as being concerned with the soldiers," and to persuade the grand jury to indict the customs agents as accessories to the murders. The publishers of the *Short Narrative*, Edes and Gill, had their office just up the street from the Old State House and practically across the street from the Court House where the grand jury sat. The publication was timely, just two weeks after the event, and barely a week after the grand jury opened its proceedings on March 13.

Prosecutor Jonathan Sewall mysteriously left town after drawing up the indictments. Radicals believed he was avoiding the case, and they demanded that a new prosecutor be appointed. His cousin Samuel Quincy, Josiah's brother, was appointed to replace him, and the town of Boston hired Robert Treat Paine, another Whig, to assist the prosecution. (Whigs were what opponents of British government policy called themselves.)

The grand jury indicted Ebenezer Richardson in the death of Christopher Seider, and it indicted Thomas Preston, William Wemms, and the seven privates for the murders of Crispus Attucks and others. But it went further. It charged four civilians—one of them a Custom House official—with firing into the crowd from inside the Custom House. The charges against these four—tide surveyor Edward Manwaring, his friend John Munroe, boatbuilder Hammond Green, and laborer Thomas Greenwood—were based on evidence supplied by Manwarring's young French servant, Charles Bourgatte.

According to Lieutenant Governor Hutchinson, the grand jury had wanted to indict the customs commissioners themselves. He wrote that "when the people are infatuated this excellent part of the English Constitution," the grand jury system, which is intended to be "a Guard to the Lives of the Innocent," was now being abused by popular pressure " to bring them into danger." Rather than protecting the innocent from a prosecutor's zeal, the grand jury itself could become a weapon of an angry public. "I am sure just now, the most innocent are the least secure."

Even though the grand jury did not indict the commissioners, Hutchinson still feared for their safety. Only one, John Temple, remained in Boston, apparently an ally of the disaffected radicals. John Paxton, Henry Hulton, and William Burch all fled to Cambridge. John Robinson, already a marked man after beating Whig James Otis in tavern encounter in 1769, left for England on March 16, carrying with him the first news of the King Street riot.

WORSE WAS TO COME for the British, in terms of propaganda. Engraver Henry Pelham made a line drawing of the event, which he titled "The Fruits of Arbitrary Power, or the Bloody Massacre." In the drawing, Pelham shows a line of seven soldiers, firing in unison at about two dozen unarmed civilians, three of whom are dead on the ground, a fourth held by his grieving friends. The civilians are not tough rope workers or sailors—and certainly not an unruly mob—but peaceable gentlemen. To underscore their pacific nature, at the feet of one victim stands his small dog, looking calmly out at the viewer. Behind the soldiers stands Colonel Preston, his sword raised in command. Though all the depositions indicated that the soldiers had their backs to the Custom House wall, Pelham takes artistic license and shows them in the middle of King Street, with the civilians with their backs to the wall on the opposite side. Most damning to the custom commissioners, Pelham has a puff of smoke issuing from a window of the Custom House.

Although Pelham could have used any perspective to show the event, he wanted us to look west, up King Street, to the Old State House. That symbol of orderly government that the troops usurped, rises silently above the scene of carnage. Rising behind the Old State House to the left is the cupola of the Old Brick Meeting House, and to the right is the Brattle Street Church. These ideals of civil government and moral authority are replaced in the streets of Boston by military force. Beneath are words from Psalm 94:

How long shall they utter and speak hard things
and all the workers of Iniquity boast themselves:

They break in pieces thy people O Lord
And afflict thine heritage:
They slay the widow and the stranger
And murder the fatherless.
Yet they say the Lord shall not see
Neither shall the God of Jacob regard it.

The psalm promises that God knows the thoughts of man, and that God will not cast off His people; "judgment shall return" to righteousness, and the upright—those who resist the evildoers—will follow.

Pelham entrusted his drawing to silversmith and coppersmith Paul Revere. Revere had produced the 1768 print on the "Landing of the British Troops," which emphasized the church steeples in Boston—and thus asked the implied question, why do such religious people need two regiments of troops to keep order? Now, with Pelham's picture in hand, Revere turned out a new engraving, which would become the most famous image of the American Revolution: "The Bloody Massacre perpetrated in King Street, Boston, on March 5th 1770 by a party of the 29th Regt." Revere's engraving is so close to Pelham's that it borders on plagiarism. The essential components are the same, though the moon is reversed and the Brattle Street steeple is not there—and Revere made some subtle but significant changes to the Custom House. The words "Butcher's Hall" are emblazoned across the front of the building, what was a puff of smoke in Pelham's engraving is a billowing cloud, and a gun protrudes from the window.

In Revere's engraving, a poem appears under the image, speaking of "faithless Preston and his savage Bands" grinning "o'er their Prey," and warning of "venal Courts," the "Scandal of the Land" that might "Snatch the relentless Villain" from the hands of earthly judges, and place him before "a Judge who never can be brib'd."

Not surprisingly, Pelham was furious with Revere, saying he thought he "had entrusted [his engraving] in the hands of a person who had more regard to the dictates of Honour and Justice than to take the undue advantage you have done of the confidence and Trust I reposed in you." Although Pelham took no legal action, he accused Revere of robbing him "as truly as if you had plundered me on the highway."

Paul Revere engraved Henry Pelham's sketch onto this copper plate, and made the image his own. (Courtesy of the Massachusetts Archives)

The engravings had the effect of fixing a particular image in the public mind: a "Bloody Massacre" perpetrated by a straight line of soldiers firing with precision into an unarmed, peaceful crowd. Revere's engraving appeared as the frontispiece to the *Short Narrative*, without a title or caption, though the first London reprinting of the *Short Narrative* included a caption that combined Pelham's and Revere's titles: "The Fruits of Arbitrary Power, or the BLOODY MASSACRE."

In answer to the *Short Narrative*, an anonymous London author in the late spring produced a pamphlet titled "A Fair Account of the Late Unhappy Disturbance at Boston in New England." What for Boston was a "Horrid Massacre" was for this writer an "Unhappy Disturbance." The pamphlet drew on depositions from the soldiers as well as from townspeople. Whereas the *Short Narrative* claimed the trouble began with the arrival of customs commissioners, the "Fair Account" begins with the fight at Gray's ropewalk. The "Fair Account"

Revere's print of the Bloody Massacre (Courtesy of the Massachusetts Archives)

renewed the popular clamor in Boston not only because its view of the events is less one-sided, but also because it contained Andrew Oliver's account of the March 6 meeting of the Governor's Council.

Oliver was secretary of the Province, and so he was responsible for public records. He was also Lieutenant Governor Thomas Hutchinson's brother-in-law (and would become lieutenant governor the next year when Hutchinson became governor), and his brother Peter had already succeeded Hutchinson as chief justice of the Superior Court. Hence Boston Whigs were deeply suspicious of Oliver's motives, recalling also that he had briefly agreed to be a Stamp Tax agent in 1765—before the Sons of Liberty had dissuaded him by demolishing his warehouse and hanging him in effigy.

According to Oliver's account published in "Fair Account," councilor Royall Tyler had said that the people of Boston had a plan to remove the troops and the customs commissioners, and Oliver implied that the radicals had this plan in place before March 5. Oliver suggested that the councilors made him change his minutes, not because he had misstated what they had said, but because they did not want their views, and their conspiracy against the law, to appear on the public record.

The councilors were furious when they read "Fair Account." In the fall of 1770 the council launched an attack on Oliver for misrepresenting what they had said in their March deliberations and for sending minutes of their discussions to London, vilolating their privilege as a deliberative body "in a secret manner" by sending the minutes to London, where they would be "made use of to represent his Majesty's Subjects here in an odious light." These secret and malicious missives had "occasioned Troops and naval armaments to be sent hither, to the great and unjust annoyance and distress of his Majesty's subjects in this Province." His faulty deposition would "give a most unfavorable and at the same time a most unjust Idea of the People here," especially the Council.

In a swift response to Andrew Oliver's words in "Fair Account," the councilors ordered a full investigation: Oliver's allegations "respecting a plan formed by the People to remove the Kings Troops and the Commissioners of Customs from the Town of Boston" would have "the most pernicious Consequences to this Province." The Council appointed five members to a committee to determine what exactly Royall Tyler had said. Had he indicated there was a preconceived plan? Had the other councilors agreed with him? Had anyone prevailed on Oliver to change the official record to reflect not what they thought but what would be politically expedient for them to think? The councilors took depositions from the previous year's council members (who were, for the most part, the same as the current year's members) and from Colonel Dalrymple and Royal Navy captain Benjamin Caldwell, two officers who had attended the tumultuous council meeting on March 6. All the councilor's depositions supported Tyler, that he had not said there was a preconceived plan to remove the troops and commissioners. Dalrymple and Caldwell were a little more ambiguous, but neither remembered that Tyler mentioned a preconceived plan to force out the commissioners. The council now said that Oliver had given a false picture of their deliberations, and furthermore that he had had no right to send minutes of these deliberations to anyone.

Andrew Oliver responded to the council that as secretary to the province, he was commissioned by the king. It was his right, if not his duty, to send minutes to the king. The council disagreed. The king had commissioned Oliver to be an officer of the Massachusetts province; his first duty as the king's servant was to the province, and if he did present information to the king he was obligated by justice and honor to make sure it was accurate. He also had a solemn obligation to inform the councilors that he was sending the king reports of their proceedings, so they could correct his mistakes and "partial Representations." By sending these secret and inaccurate minutes, Oliver had betrayed the king and the province, and his actions threatened to "degrade him into the character of a Spy and an Informer." His actions were "subversive of every principle which distinguishes a free government from Despotism."

At the end of October 1770, the Governor's Council agreed unanimously that Andrew Oliver had committed a breach of trust, had violated the privileges of the council and threatened its freedom of debate, had injured individual councilors and brought great dishonor on the council as a whole. The council sent its report to its own agent in England, to take appropriate action.

WHETHER THE EVENTS OF THE EVENING of March 5 were a "Horrid Massacre," in the view of the town, or an "Unhappy Disturbance," as the London pamphlet called it, by the end of 1770 it had the town of Boston, the Massachusetts Assembly, and the Governor's Council all firmly on one side, and Governor Thomas Hutchinson and Secretary Andrew Oliver on the other. Hutchinson knew that the protests were not aimed at him personally but were part of the general resistance to parliamentary authority. Though Bostonians were using the aftermath of the massacre against Hutchinson and Oliver, their real target was the government of England that the two men represented. Knowing the situation was unraveling, Hutchinson wrote to Lord Hillsborough that "the authority of Government is gone," and that he did not have the "strength of constitution to withstand the whole force of the Government united against the Governor in every measure."

The Verdicts of the Courts

THE TRAGIC EVENTS OF MARCH 5 were part of a political struggle and would have dramatic political consequences. But the shooting deaths of five colonists also presented a legal issue. Lieutenant Governor Hutchinson had pledged to "live and die by the law," and the main reason he spent the long night of March 5 interviewing witnesses was to establish whether criminal charges should be filed. Captain Thomas Preston testified for an hour in the council chamber in the wee hours of Tuesday, March 6. By three o'clock that morning, he was en route to jail. Corporal Wemms and the seven soldiers were in jail before noon.

The jail at the courthouse was the safest place for the soldiers, as some Bostonians were ready to lynch them. Would it be possible to find a lawyer in Boston willing to represent them? Preston feared that he was "at the mercy of a partial jury, whose prejudice is kept up by a set of designing villains, that only draw their subsistence from the disturbance they cause."

James Forrest, an Irish merchant in Boston who had befriended Preston, immediately took it upon himself to find able counsel. He first went to Josiah Quincy, regarded as one of the leading lights among the Whigs. Josiah's brother Samuel, who would prosecute the soldiers on behalf of the British crown, had called his younger brother Josiah "a WILKES of Spirit and Abilities, equal to the Government." Given that Samuel was a loyalist, the comparison to John Wilkes, a leading British radical he deemed a troublemaker and traitor, was hardly a compliment. But James Forrest knew both Josiah Quincy's legal abilities and his politics; in his view, only a Whig, an opponent of British government policies, could defend the soldiers who had killed civilians in defense of those policies.

Quincy agreed to represent Preston and the soldiers, he told Forrest, but only if Forrest could persuade John Adams to assist him. John Adams, cousin of the radical leader Samuel Adams, was becoming known as one of the best young lawyers in Boston, and also one of the foremost Whigs. Forrest immediately went to Adams's law office, near the steps of the Old State House. While Hutchinson and the Council were meeting just across the way, and the town meeting was taking place at Old South, John Adams was in his law office when Forrest came in and said, "I come with a very solemn Message from a very unfortunate Man, Captain Preston in Prison. He wishes for Council, and can get none."

Forrest said he had spoken with Quincy, who would take Preston's case if Adams would assist him. Robert Auchmuty, Jr., had also declined to represent Preston unless Adams would join them. "I had no hesitation in answering that Council ought to be the very last thing that an accused Person should want in a free Country," Adams remembered answering, though he wrote this recollection in 1816. By giving Preston and the soldiers a fair trial, Adams could demonstrate that Boston was not in the hands of a lawless mob, but that impartial justice would still be served.

While three thousand of their townsmen were meeting at Old South demanding the immediate removal of the troops, and ten thousand people in Charlestown, Roxbury, Dorchester, and Braintree were threatening to occupy the Common to protect Bostonians from the murderous British soldiers, Josiah Quincy, John Adams, and Robert Auchmuty prepared to defend Preston and the soldiers. Adams remembered telling Forrest, "Every Lawyer must hold himself responsible not only to his Country, but to the highest and most infallible of all Trybunals for the Part he should Act." For these reasons, Preston should expect from Adams "no Art or Address, No Sophistry or Prevarication in such a Cause; nor any thing more than Fact, Evidence and Law would justify." Preston's guilt or innocence "must be ascertained by his Tryal."

Josiah Quincy (1744–1775) defended Preston and the British soldiers. Gilbert Stuart painted this portrait in the 1820s, at the request of Quincy's son, Boston Mayor Josiah Quincy. (Courtesy of the Museum of Fine Arts, Boston)

Josiah Quincy's father was distraught when he heard that his son would be defending British soldiers. "I am under great affliction," he wrote his son, "hearing the bitterest reproaches against you." Men who had previously thought the younger Quincy was "destined to be a saviour for your country" now made the "severest reflections" on him. It filled "the bosom of your aged and infirm parent with anxiety and distress," worrying that it might be true, and that it would destroy his "reputation and interest."

Josiah replied that he had neither time nor inclination to respond to "ignorant slanderers" who criticized him for defending "criminals charged with murder." His true friends would reflect "on the nature of an attorney's oath and duty" before "pouring their reproaches" into his father's ear. Captain Preston and his soldiers "are not yet legally proved guilty," he emphasized, and so they were entitled "by the laws of God and man, to all legal counsel and aid," which Josiah Quincy's duty as a man and a lawyer required him to give. Quincy told his father that he had at first declined to take the case, but on the advice of "an Adams, a Hancock, a Molineux, a Cushing, a Henshaw, a Pemberton, a Warren, a Cooper, and a Phillips"—that is, of all the leading Whigs in Boston—he had changed his mind. He had also met with Preston, and in the presence of two of Preston's friends "made the most explicit declaration . . .

John Adams (1735–1826) defended Preston and the British soldiers. Benjamin Blyth painted Adams as a young lawyer a few years before the trial. (Courtesy of the Massachusetts Historical Society)

of my real opinion on the contests . . . of the times." Though he would defend Preston and the soldiers, "my heart and hand were indissolubly attached to the cause of my country." Quincy predicted that "this whole people will one day REJOICE that I became an advocate for the aforesaid 'criminals' charged with the murder of our fellow-citizens."

Quincy and Adams would not have an easy time defending these men. Not only was the temper of the people set firmly against their clients, so was the weight of the evidence. As General Thomas Gage wrote from New York, "It is much to be feared the Prisoners will not be tried by a fair and unprejudiced Jury, and that the very People who assaulted them will be brought as Evidence against them." As Adams and Quincy began to prepare their defense, the town of Boston was busy building its case against the soldiers in the court of public opinion.

The Superior Court session began at the end of March, when the trial would have been expected to begin. But with two of the four judges ill, the others decided to adjourn until June. The judges hoped to delay the trial of the soldiers, and of Ebenezer Richardson, as long as they could. But before they could adjourn, in came Samuel Adams, William Molineux, Joseph Warren, John Hancock, and "a vast concourse of people after them" representing the town of Boston, and Adams "harangued the judges" making "a very pathetic Speech," according to Judge Oliver, "Represented the necessity of proceeding to the trial . . . , particularly those concerned in the late bloody Massacre."

Samuel Adams had shrewdly kept Boston's town meeting in session, merely adjourning it from day to day, so that he would have an official position from which to "observe how the business of the court goes on." On March 19, the town formally asked Lieutenant Governor Hutchinson and the council to appoint special judges to fill in for those who were ill.

Hutchinson himself had been chief justice since 1760; now that Hutchinson was acting governor, awaiting his appointment to succeed

Peter Oliver (1713–1791) succeeded his in-law Thomas Hutchinson as Chief Justice. After he fled to England in 1776, Oliver wrote his **Origin and Progress of the American Rebellion.** *(Courtesy of the Museum of Fine Arts, Boston)*

Bernard, Judge Benjamin Lynde presided over the court. Lynde was approaching seventy, and the prospect of presiding over these contentious trials prompted him to offer his resignation—twice. Hutchinson refused it—twice. Lynde was a timid man, but the other judges were even more so. Hutchinson knew that "Little matters as well as great frighten Lynde," but Judge Edmund Trowbridge "appears valiant until the danger or apprehensions of it, rise to considerable height, after that he is more terrified than the other."

Of the other two judges, Peter Oliver, Andrew's younger brother, "appears to be very firm." Hutchinson hoped that John Cushing "will be so likewise." These imperfect men, with all their flaws, gave justice a better chance of being done "than with any new Judges I could have appointed who would have accepted."

To appease the town and delay the trials of Preston and the soldiers, the court set an earlier trial for Ebenezer Richardson and George Wilmot, charged in the death of Christopher Seider on February 22. Judge Oliver wrote that "had a trial been refused, it was rather more than an equal chance that the Prisoners," Preston, the soldiers, and Ebenezer Richardson, "would have been murdered by the Rabble; and the judges been exposed to Assassinations." On Monday, March 19, the court arraigned Richardson for murder, and charged Wilmot as an accomplice, and set their trial date for the following Friday. Richardson appeared that Friday but asked for a postponement—though he "had made application to almost every Lawyer in town," none would represent him; the constables "had refused summoning his witnesses," and the jailer had prevented him from talking with any who might aid him. Also "every Newspaper was crouded with the most infamous and false libels against him in order to prejudice the minds of his jury." The judges agreed to postpone the trial, and appointed Samuel Fitch, newly appointed advocate for the Vice Admiralty Court, to defend Richardson. Fitch, an ally of the customs establishment, tried to get out of the assignment, but the judges ordered him to defend Richardson.

The court postponed the trial again until April 17. Fitch was too ill to attend, so the court appointed Josiah Quincy, who was already defending Preston and the soldiers, to defend Richardson and Wilmot. Quincy, "actuated solely from the motive of humanity," and "without fee or reward, and at the hazard of losing his popular reputation," took a courageous step in defending Richardson. Sampson Salter Blowers, his college classmate, assisted Quincy, while Quincy's brother Samuel and Robert Treat Paine presented the case for the prosecution. The trial began and ended on Friday, April 20. As he later would in the cases of Preston, Weems, and seven privates, Josiah Quincy presented evidence that Richardson and Wilmot were under assault, Richardson's house was being attacked by a mob, and that therefore he was justified in firing his weapon.

It was a reasonable argument, but neither the jury nor the crowd in the courtroom accepted it. While one of judges instructed the jurors that the verdict should be justifiable homicide, a spectator shouted, "Damn that Judge, if I was nigh him, I would give it to him." Judge Oliver noted that "this was not a Time, to attempt to preserve Decorum; Preservation of Life was as much as a Judge dared aim at."

The crowds inside the court and out intimidated the jurors, reminding them that "you are upon Oath," and that "Blood requires blood." Men stood at the door holding a noose, preparing to lynch Richardson when he was brought out of the court. To prevent that, the judges had him locked in the courtroom until the crowd dispersed, and they themselves waited an hour for the crowd to thin before they ventured outside, to the sustained hissing of remaining onlookers.

The jurors deliberated all night, from eleven o'clock until eight or nine o'clock the next morning. Richardson was guilty, Wilmot not guilty. "An universal clap ensued" when Richardson's verdict was announced, and the spectators cheered. But the judges knew the verdict defied the law; Quincy and Blowers had proved that Richardson, however odious an individual, was under attack on February 22. The court and Hutchinson then began a process of delay so that the king could pardon Richardson before the Boston authorities had to hang him. Finally, in September, the court heard testimony from the jurors about how they had arrived at the verdict under fear of the mob, and Blowers argued that the verdict should be set aside. Hutchinson wrote to Lord Hillsborough, recommending a pardon for Richardson, who remained in jail. In the meantime, with Richardson convicted, the town of Boston was demanding trials for the soldiers. The court delayed scheduling the trial for as long as possible, hoping that tempers might cool, but Revere's engraving appearing everywhere, and constant agitation by the Sons of

Liberty made public pressure overwhelming. Finally, on September 7, the day before the court adjourned until late October, it brought charges against Preston, Wemms, and the seven privates. All pleaded not guilty. When the court opened its fall session in Boston on October 24, its first task was the trial of Thomas Preston. Preston's trial was the first in memory that lasted more than a day; each night the jury was sequestered in the jail. "I know," Peter Oliver wrote to Thomas Hutchinson at the end of the trial, "you think you would have finished the Cause in half the Time and I know it would not have taken half a day at the Old Bailey; but we must conform to the Times."

No reliable transcript of the Preston trial remains. We know from Preston's letters that he thought the prosecution lawyers "for the Crown or rather the town" were "poor and managed poorly," and that Robert Treat Paine was too ill to finish his argument on time. But Preston was impressed with his own defense counsel, particularly Robert Auchmuty, who finished his closing arguments at four-thirty on Saturday, October 27. The court adjourned until Monday morning, leaving the jurors locked in the courthouse on Sunday.

At noon on Monday, the judges began their instructions to the jury. Judge Trowbridge's charge, printed later that year in London's *Annual Register*, said that to him the evidence did not show "that the prisoner gave the orders to fire." If so, what was Preston's crime? Was it murder? Trowbridge did not think so, as the king had a right to send his troops to Boston; the commanding officer had a right to station a sentinel at the Custom House; the sentinel could not quit his post; if he was insulted or attacked, the captain had a right to protect him. Further, while Preston and the soldiers were within their rights and "in the King's peace," a great number of people, "not in the King's peace, but . . . by law considered as a riotous mob" had attacked them with ice, sticks, and clubs. One witness (Benjamin Burdick) confessed that he had carried a Highland broadsword while shouting, "Knock them down! Kill them! Kill them!"

Trowbridge explained that if Preston was guilty of any crime, it was excusable homicide, but only if he had given the order to fire. After Trowbridge, Judge Peter Oliver spoke in "a very nervous and pathetic manner" of the "insults and outrages" he and the court had received for their actions in the Richardson trial. Despite this, and despite all that had been "done to prejudice the People against the Prisoner"—particularly a "copper Plate Print [Paul Revere's engraving] . . . in which this Court has been insulted and call'd a venal Court, if this Prisoner was not condemned"—Oliver would do his duty.

The judges turned the case over to the jury at five that afternoon. The jurors deliberated for three hours, then were sequestered for the night. At eight the next morning they acquitted Captain Preston, who took refuge at Castle William to avoid trouble in the town.

General Thomas Gage had hoped that the same jury that acquitted Preston would also hear the soldiers' case, but the court adjourned and the soldiers would not be tried for nearly a month. The town wanted to prepare better for this trial, and Robert Treat Paine was instructed to come to Boston to work with Samuel Quincy. Samuel Adams also made himself available to assist the prosecution, and he attended the trial to advise Quincy and Paine.

The case of Rex v. Wemms opened on Tuesday, November 27, 1770. The soldiers were all identified in the indictments as "labourers," and it is doubtful that they would have worn their uniforms to trial. They had been in jail since March, and now, according to the custom, they stood each day in the prisoner's dock of the courtroom.

The jurors were chosen—two from Roxbury, two from Dorchester, and the rest from towns no longer part of Suffolk County: Hingham, Milton, Stoughton, Braintree, and Dedham. No Bostonians were chosen. One juror was excused for having said that though Preston was innocent, someone should hang for shedding innocent blood. Like Preston's trial, the soldiers' trial lasted more than a day, with jurors sequestered in the courthouse overnight.

Witnesses for the prosecution testified that the accused had fired, that the soldiers at Corn Hill had been provoking the townspeople, that Matthew Kilroy's bayonet had been examined the next day and found covered with blood. Five witnesses saw Hugh Montgomery fire, and four testified that Hugh White had fired. Three witnesses saw Kilroy fire, and Sheriff Stephen Greenleaf's coachman, Samuel Hemmingway, remembered a conversation about a week or two before March 5, in which Kilroy had said he "would never miss an opportunity, when he had one, to fire on the inhabitants." On cross-examination, Hemmingway said that Kilroy was neither angry nor drunk, but he could not say

Samuel Quincy (1735–1789), Josiah's older brother, led the prosecution of Preston, Wemms, and the soldiers. He remained loyal to the king and empire and spent his last years practicing law in the British West Indies. (Courtesy of the Museum of Fine Arts, Boston)

if it was "jocular talk." Three witnesses saw William Warren fire, though one of them expressed some doubt, and two witnesses accused James Hartigan, John Carroll, and William Wemms of firing. Only one witness, John Adams's clerk, saw William McCauley fire his gun.

Friday morning Samuel Quincy concluded the prosecution's case, and his brother Josiah opened the case for the defense. He reminded the jurors that they were "not sitting here as statesmen or Politicians." As jurors, they had "nothing to do with the Injuries your Country has sustained. The Town is not concerned." Josiah Quincy knew the case had "awakened the Attention of the whole Continent if not all Europe," but the jurors should be careful "to give a Verdict, which will bear the Examination of Times, when the Pulses which now beat shall beat no more."

Quincy warned the jurors not to be "led away" by their political beliefs. The prisoners could be convicted only by evidence that appeared in court, not by evidence that "has appeared in the world against us." He told them that the town's *Short Narrative*, with its depositions, was not enough. None of those witnesses had been cross-examined, and though all "the colours of the canvass have been touched in order to freshen the wounds," and the vivid prose "by a transport of imagination" makes us seem to be "present at the scene of action," the story told in the *Short Narrative* was not credible evidence in court. "The prints exhibited in our houses have added wings to fancy," he said of the Revere and Pelham prints. But these images distorted the "pomp of funerals" for the victims, the "horrors of death have been so delineated, as to give a spring to our ideas," and aroused a "torrent of passion" that would "make a shipwreck of conscience."

Josiah Quincy very briefly narrated the history of the troubles between Britain and its colonies, and the passions and resentment on both sides. Then he turned to the prosecution's evidence, focusing on that which showed an assault on the sentry. He called his witnesses, who reported the streets alive with people armed with clubs, sticks, and swords, the attack on Murray's Barracks, the cries of fire. The prosecution had depicted a Boston seething under the British occupation, with soldiers insulting inhabitants at every turn. Josiah Quincy presented a much different picture of Boston on the evening of March 5. The streets were teeming with armed citizens looking for trouble. With this vivid picture, Quincy closed his arguments for the day, and the court adjourned.

The next morning, Dr. Richard Hirons, who lived across the street from Murray's Barracks, testified about the fight there. Next the defense called Captain Goldfinch, who recalled how he had ordered the soldiers inside after the riot. Andrew, a slave to merchant Oliver Wendell, testified that he saw numbers of boys throwing snowballs at the sentinels in front of the Main Guard. They insulted the red-uniformed soldiers by calling them "lobsters, bloody backs," shouting "Who buys lobsters?" to taunt the soldiers, referring to their red uniforms and to the floggings they endured as part of British military discipline. Lobsters were scavengers, feeding on the garbage which would accumulate under Boston's wharves. Andrew said that his friend had told him about the fight at Murray's Barracks, and he saw the crowd coming around the Brazen Head tavern into King Street, and he also saw people picking up chunks of coal and snow to throw at the sentinel at the Custom House. Then he saw an officer and line of soldiers march toward the Custom House. They did not get out of formation, Andrew said. "[I]f they had they might have killed me and many others with their bayonets."

Andrew got as close as he could to the soldiers in front of the Custom. He saw a man talking to the officer, and someone turned to tell the crowd, "Damn him he is going to fire." The crowd shouted back, "Fire and be damn'd, who cares, damn you, you dare not fire." The crowd began to throw snowballs and other things, "which then flew pretty thick." The soldiers tried to push the people away, as the snow and rocks hit them. Andrew thought the crowd was beginning to turn away when another raucous contingent, led by a man Andrew identified as Crispus Attucks, carrying a big stick, came down from Jackson's corner "huzzaing and crying Damn them they dare not fire we are not afraid of them." Attucks struck at the officer, Andrew reported, and then knocked the gun from Kilroy's hand, holding the bayonet and crying, "Kill the dogs, knock them over," as the crowd pressed in closer to the soldiers. Andrew got out of the crowd at this time, turning back when he heard a shot. After the shot he heard the word *fire*.

Andrew described a melee, not a peaceable gathering. Now, Quincy asked, did he see "a number of people take up any and every thing they could find in the street, and throw them at the soldiers?"

"Yes, I saw ten or fifteen round me do it."

"Did you yourself pick up everything you could find, and throw at them?"

"Yes, I did."

Andrew's master, Oliver Wendell, testified that Andrew had told him this same story about fifteen minutes after the events on King Street, that "and then I asked him whether our people were to blame, and he said they were." Wendell knew Andrew had "a lively imagination" but he "never knew him to tell a serious lye." Bricklayer William Parker testified that he saw seven or eight boys—eighteen years old—tearing apart butchers' stalls in Faneuil Hall for clubs, and when they spotted an officer they cried, "Here is a damned soldier" and attacked him, but Parker was able to get the man away.

Dr. John Jeffries testified that he had been at his father's home across from the Brattle Square Church during the riot at Murray's Barracks. When "the girl ran in from the kitchen and said there is a gun fired," Jeffries said he did not believe it. He had already seen the officers at Murray's barracks "put in the soldiers and shut the gate." However, Jeffries's more crucial testimony was his account of the dying words of Patrick Carr. Jeffries had gone to care for Carr beginning on March 7, and he continued to care for him until his death the following week.

During that time, Jeffries asked Carr if he had thought the soldiers would fire.

"He told me he thought the soldiers would have fired long before," Jeffries said, in testimony that carried great weight because Carr was a victim. "I asked him whether the soldiers were abused a great deal, after they went down there? He said, he thought they were. I asked him whether he thought the soldiers would have been hurt, if they had not fired? He said he really thought they would, for he heard many voices cry out, kill them." According to Jeffries, Carr said he thought the soldiers were in danger, and he "did not blame the man whoever he was, that shot him."

Every time he called on Carr, Jeffries said, the wounded man gave the same answers. Carr also told Jeffries that back in his native Ireland "he had frequently seen mobs, and soldiers called upon to quell them." Carr called himself a fool, that he "might have known better, that he had seen soldiers often fire on the people in Ireland, but had never seen them bear half so much before they fired in his life." This kind of dying declaration is still admissible as evidence, an exception to the legal rule about hearsay. Jeffries reported that he saw Carr for the last time just a few hours before he died, and Carr "forgave the man whoever he was that shot him, he was satisfied he had no malice, but fired to defend himself."

JOSIAH QUINCY CLOSED HIS ARGUMENTS for the defense on Monday, December 3. He repeated much of what he had said in his opening, drawing a distinction between the soldiers who had rioted at Murray's Barracks on Corn Hill and those who stood accused of murder. Then he then turned the defense over to John Adams.

Adams began by referring to the popular clamor against the soldiers. He invoked Italian jurist Cesare Beccaria's *Essay on Crimes and Punishments*, saying that if he could "be the instrument of preserving one life," it would make up "for the contempt of all mankind." Far better that "many guilty persons should escape unpunished, than that one innocent person should suffer." A community, Adams said, gained more by protecting innocence than by punishing guilt.

In clear and plain language, Adams explained the different kinds homicides and assaults, and then he applied these definitions to the case at hand. Suppose, he asked, that Colonel Thomas Marshall, who lived next door to the Custom House, had come out of his house to see the soldiers marching toward him "with swords &c.," and suppose Marshall had "assembled [Samuel] Gray and Attucks that were killed" and made them into a military watch, and that "three or forty soldiers, with no other arms than snowballs, cakes of ice, oyster shells, cinders and clubs," attacked them? What would have been Gray's and Attucks's reactions? Adams did not believe that Gray and Attucks would have "borne the one half" of what the soldiers had "till they had shot down as many as were necessary to intimidate and disperse the rest." The law does not "oblige us to bear insults to the danger of our lives, to stand still with such a number of people round us, throwing such things at us" until we can no longer defend ourselves.

Adams built on the testimony that had shown the assembly on King Street to be a riot. Riots happen in any government, even in the mildest, since "the people are liable to run into riots and tumults." Riots are more likely in despotisms than in republics, but "such is the imperfection of all things in this world, that no form of government, and perhaps no wisdom or virtue in the administration, can at all times avoid riots and disorders among the people." But while riots happened, Adams explained, the law discouraged them "because once they begin, there is danger of their running to such excesses, as will overturn the whole system of government."

Adams quoted an English legal text that defined rioters as "more than three persons" using force or violence to accomplish an end, and anyone involved in a riot as a principal to any murder the mob committed. "Were there not more than three persons in Dock-Square? Did they not agree to go to King-street, and attack the Main guard? Where then, is the reason for hesitation, at calling it a riot? If we cannot speak the law as it is, where is our liberty?"

Sheriffs, magistrates, and even private persons could gather a force to suppress or "oppose rebels, enemies, or rioters." Adams took a step back to say, "I do not mean to apply the word *rebel* on this occasion: I have no reason to suppose that ever there was one in Boston, at least among the natives of the country." The mob on King Street were not rebels, and Adams wanted to make clear while there had been a riot, Bostonians were not rebellious.

Adams said that if the prisoners were not considered as soldiers but as "neighbours," and if their neighbors "were attacked in King-street, they had a right to collect together to suppress this riot and combination." How far was a neighbor empowered to aid another in distress? "Suppose a press gang should come ashore in this town, and assault any sailor, or householder in King street, in order to carry them on board one of his Majesty's ships and impress him without warrant . . . how far do you suppose the inhabitants would think themselves warranted by law, to interpose against that lawless press gang?"

This was a brilliant analogy; no doubt the members of the jury remembered the attempt by the HMS *Preston*, in 1748, to impress Bostonians into the navy; the press gang came up King Street but was surrounded by Bostonians who prevented them from taking any into service. Now, Adams said, "Such a press gang would be as unlawful an assembly, as that was in King street. If they were to press an inhabitant, . . . would not the inhabitants think themselves warranted by law to interpose in behalf of their fellow citizens?" But if these soldiers on trial did not have the right to defend the sentry, then the inhabitants would have no right to defend a citizen, "for whatever is law for a soldier, is law for a sailor, and for a citizen, they all stand upon an equal footing, in this respect."

Adams went through the witnesses, particularly those for the prosecution, showing how all the testimony agreed there was a violent, unlawful assembly on the night of March 5. He spent much time on the testimony of the constable Edward Langford, who had seen twenty or twenty-five teenage boys surrounding Hugh White, and who had told the sentry not to be afraid. Why, Adams asked, would Langford have told White not to be afraid unless "there was danger, or at least that the Sentinel in fact, was terrified and did think himself in danger." Langford called the boys "young shavers," provoking Adams to say, "We have been entertained with a great variety of phrases, to avoid calling this sort of people a mob.—Some call them shavers, some call them genius's.—The plain English is, gentlemen, most probably a motley rabble of saucy boys, negroes and mulattos, Irish teagues and outlandish jack tarrs. "

Why would "such a set of people" not be called a mob, "unless the name is too respectable for them:—The sun is not about to stand still or go out, nor the rivers to dry up because there was a mob in Boston on the 5th of March that attacked a party of soldiers." Though mobs were rare in Boston, they could be expected since "soldiers quartered in a populous town, will always occasion two mobs, where they prevent one.—They are wretched conservators of the peace!"

Returning to Langford's deposition, Adams noted the "rattling" the constable had heard as the ice struck the soldiers' guns. Other witnesses also had heard this rattling.

Forty or fifty people around the soldiers, and more coming from Quaker-Lane, as well as the other lanes. The soldiers heard all the bells ringing and saw people coming from every point of the compass to the assistance of those who were insulting, assaulting, beating and abusing of them—what had they to expect but destruction, if they had not thus early taken measures to defend themselves?

With this crowd "shouting and huzzaing, and threatening life, the bells all ringing, the mob whistle screaming and rending like an Indian yell, the people from all quarters throwing every species of rubbish they could pick up in the street, . . . throwing clubs at the whole party," when Hugh Montgomery was hit "with a club and knocked down, and as soon as he could rise" another club "struck his breast or shoulder, what could he do?" Adams asked. "Do you expect he should behave like a Stoick Philosopher lost in Apathy?"

The sailor James Bailey and the slave Andrew both saw Crispus Attucks coming on the attack. Bailey saw him "at the head of twenty or thirty sailors in Corn-hill, and he had a large cordwood stick."

[Attucks] appears to have undertaken to be the hero of the night, and to lead this army with banners, to form them in the first place in Dock Square, and march them up King Street, with their clubs. If this was not an unlawful assembly, there never was one in the world. Attucks with his myrmidons comes round Jackson's corner, and down to the party by the Sentry-box; when the soldiers pushed the people off, this man with his party cried, do not be afraid of them, they dare not fire, kill them! Kill them! Knock them over! And he tried to knock their brains out.

The soldiers stood their ground, but now faced "this reinforcement under the command of a stout Molatto fellow, whose very looks was enough to terrify any person." Attucks took hold of a bayonet with one hand, and with the other he knocked the soldier down.

This was the behavior of Attucks:—to whose mad behaviour, in all probability, the dreadful carnage of that night, is chiefly to be ascribed. And it is in this manner, this town has been often treated; a Carr from Ireland, and an Attucks from Framingham, happening to be here, shall sally out upon their thoughtless enterprises, at the head of such a rabble of Negroes &c., as they can collect together, and then there are not wanting persons to ascribe all their doings to the good people of the town.

With his dramatic description of the riot, John Adams was absolving native Bostonians of responsibility. The riot was the work of these outsiders—Carr and Attucks—and not the natural result of the lawlessness that Governor Bernard had said made the troops necessary. In his summation, he had masterfully presented the story of the events of March 5, painting the mob, led by Attucks, as a dangerous force, while absolving the "good people of the town" from the charge of lawlessness. The troops had in fact provoked the riot—standing armies, as he said, created two mobs where they suppress one—but the soldiers under attack had the right to defend themselves.

"I will enlarge no more on the evidence," Adams said, "but submit it to you. Facts are stubborn things; and whatever may be our wishes, our inclinations, or the dictates of our passions, they cannot alter the state of facts and evidence." The law was clear. If the soldiers had been assaulted, and their lives were endangered, "they had a right to kill in their own defence." If the assault did not endanger their lives, but they were struck by snowballs, oyster shells, cinders, clubs, and sticks—then this was provocation enough to reduce their offense to manslaughter.

Having begun by invoking Beccaria, Adams concluded by citing the English libertarian Algernon Sydney, "enlightened friend of mankind, and a martyr to liberty," who had said the law was void of desire and fear, lust and anger, but punishes the guilty "whether rich, or poor, or high, or low," Adams concluded. "On the one hand," the law "is inexorable to the cries and lamentations of the prisoners; on the other it is deaf, deaf as an adder to the clamours of the populace."

In offering the prosecution's closing argument, which he had to continue the next morning, Wednesday, December 5, Robert Treat Paine had the difficult task of following John Adams's summation. He argued that the people of Boston were within their rights to be out on such a pleasant night and had armed themselves because of provocations from the troops. Why had Patrick Carr and so many other Bostonians come out armed? It was because "a number of soldiers had come out of their barracks armed with clubs, bayonets, cutlasses, and tongs. In the most disorderly and outrageous manner they were ravaging the streets, assaulting everyone they met, turning out of their way to assault and endanger the lives of peaceable inhabitants." According to Paine, the soldiers themselves constituted an unlawful assembly. He also focused attention directly on Montgomery and Kilroy. Montgomery had been knocked down, and so his crime in killing Attucks might be manslaughter, but what about Kilroy who had shot Gray? Had he been provoked? Had any of the other soldiers? "Shall throwing a snowball from a distance alleviate the crime of firing a musketball amidst a crowd of people who at first stood so thick they could not throw?" Adams had insisted that facts were stubborn things; Paine stuck with the facts. Just as Adams charged that all in the mob were responsible for violence done by the mob, so each of the soldiers was "answerable for the doings of the rest."

After Paine finished, the justices—Edmund Trowbridge, Peter Oliver, John Cushing, and Benjamin Lynde charged the jury. Oliver pointed out that there were five victims, but eight defendants. Could all the defendants be responsible for shooting all the victims? He also criticized the "attempts to prejudice the minds of the good people of this province against the prisoners at the bar," and those "persons among us who have endeavoured to bring this Supreme Court of Law into contempt, and even to destroy the Law itself." He warned that there would come a time when "those persons themselves may want the protection of the law and of this Court, which they now endeavour to destroy."

The jury began to deliberate at half past one. By four o'clock they were done. Foreman Joseph Mayo of Roxbury read the verdicts.

Corporal Wemms, James Hartigan, William McCauley, Hugh White, William Warren, and John Carroll, not guilty. Hugh Montgomery and Matthew Kilroy, not guilty of murder, but guilty of manslaughter.

The acquitted, having spent eight months in jail, were released immediately.. Montgomery and Kilroy, though cleared of murder, could still hang for manslaughter. To spare them from hanging, John Adams pleaded "benefit of clergy," a medieval protection extended to priests in England, who could be tried by ecclesiastical but not secular courts. Clergy then had been among the few able to read, so a literate convicted of manslaughter could plead benefit of clergy. By the eighteenth century this legal protection was extended in manslaughter cases even to illiterates, but could only be used once. To ensure that the benefit of clergy would not be used again, the convict would be branded on the thumb. On December 14 Kilroy and Montgomery had their thumbs branded and then were released. The men now rejoined their unit, which had been sent to New Jersey, and Preston sailed for England.

While the soldiers now were free, Boston was not through looking for scapegoats. On December 12 the court heard the case of the men charged with firing out of the Custom House on March 5. Samuel Quincy once again handled the prosecution, without assistance, and again he thought he "came off . . . like poor Quixot" in this "Windmill adventure." The defendants—Edward Manwaring, John Munroe, Hammond Green, and Thomas Greenwood—apparently acted as their own counselors.

Though the *Short Narrative* emphasized that a gun fired from the Custom House, and Revere's engraving showed a gun in the window, at the trial itself only two witnesses could positively testify to this. The first was Samuel Drowne, who said he saw a person on the Custom House balcony holding something like a gun, and he saw the gun flash. After the soldiers fired, the man went inside, stooping, and Drowne saw a flash from another window.

The other witness was Manwaring's servant Charles Bourgatte, a French boy from Bordeaux. Bourgatte said he had been at his master's lodgings in the North End, had run to King Street when he heard the bells, and Hammond Green had pulled him into the Custom House. Manwaring was inside, with a "tall man" who gave Bourgatte a gun and ordered him to fire. The tall man repeatedly told Bourgatte that "if you don't fire I will kill you." He fired, and Manwaring also fired. Though the tall man told Bourgatte he would pay him to keep quiet, Bourgatte refused, saying that if he was "called before the Justices, I would tell the truth." He left the Custom House and returned to the North End.

Bourgatte's story did not hold up. None of the witnesses who had stood across King Street had seen any guns fired from the Custom House. The wife of Manwaring's landlord, Elizabeth Hudson, testified that Manwaring, Munroe, and Bourgatte were at home all evening on March 5. Two women who lived in the Custom House, Elizabeth Avery and Ann Green, said they had not opened the windows, there were no guns in the house, and neither Manwaring nor Munroe was there that evening. As for Greenwood, Avery did not "ever see him there in my life."

James Penny, who was imprisoned for debt at the same time as Bourgatte back in March, testified that Bourgatte had told him that all of his grand jury testimony was false, that radical leader William Molineux had told Bourgatte that if he testified against Manwaring, he would be freed from his indenture and provided for, but if he backed out "the mob in Boston would kill him." Molineux had also taken Bourgatte out of jail to the North End home of Mrs. Waldron, who gave the boy "ginger bread and cheese, and desired him to swear against his master."

The jurors did not even leave their seats to acquit the defendants. Bourgatte was held; he was indicted for perjury, and in the spring of 1771 sentenced to an hour in the pillory and twenty-five lashes. The Sons of Liberty prevented the sentence from being carried out on the first attempt, but on March 28, 1771, he was put in the stocks across King Street from the site of the bloody events of March 5. His punishment was the most severe handed out for the events of that fateful night.

The Verdicts of History

"ALL THE BELLS IN TOWN ARE NOW TOLLING," Thomas Hutchinson wrote on March 5, 1771, "to show that the persons who have the direction of the Town differ from the Law in their construction of the Return this Day twelve Months." Hutchinson believed the jury's verdict had ended the controversy over that terrible night of March 5, 1770. But he was wrong. He was, however, right that there were people in town determined to keep the memory of March 5 alive, and to use it in their continuing campaign against British rule. And long after the campaign against the British had been won, the memory of the Boston Massacre continued to be revived and its lessons taught anew.

That evening Dr. Thomas Young delivered a commemorative lecture at the Manufactory House, the scene of the first conflict between the British soldiers and Boston's townspeople. At the Manufactory House in 1768, as at King Street in 1770, the British soldiers had encountered Boston's poor. Each time the poor citizens had refused to yield to military power. As Young gave an account of the massacre, he discussed the charges of treason being leveled against the townspeople, and he asserted that the real treason was the threat to take away the Massachusetts provincial charter.

Between nine and ten o'clock that evening the church bells tolled, and Paul Revere illuminated his windows on North Square with scenes of the massacre. The first window showed the ghost of Christopher Seider trying to stop the blood pouring from his wounds. Also in the image was a pyramid with Seider's name on the top and those of Attucks, Caldwell, Carr, Maverick, and Gray around the base, and two lines of poetry below, which reminded the reader that Ebenezer Richardson, though convicted, had not been executed:

Snider's pale ghost fresh bleeding stands
And vengeance for his death demands.

In the far window sat the female figure of "AMERICA" on a tree stump, holding a staff with a liberty cap atop it, her foot planted on the head of prostrate British grenadier who clutched a snake. "America" pointed to the middle window, where, under the title "FOUL PLAY," Revere had illuminated a scene of the massacre—the soldiers drawn up in formation firing at the crowd, blood streaming from the victims' wounds.

Thomas Young the orator and Paul Revere the artist both belonged to the Sons of Liberty (or, as one of Hutchinson's correspondents called them, "those Sons of Violence"), who arranged these displays, which in turn compelled the town of Boston to plan its own appropriate commemoration. At the annual town meeting on March 19, it was decided that Latin School usher James Lovell should deliver a memorial oration on April 2 at Faneuil Hall. So many people turned out that the event was moved to Old South Meeting House. Calling himself "an American son of liberty," Lovell urged Bostonians to "make the bloody fifth of March the era of the resurrection of your birthrights, which have been murdered by the very strength that nursed them in their infancy!"

In a letter to Lord Hillsborough, Hutchinson mentioned the oration, which was

> pronounced in one of the Meeting houses to a crowded Audience, to commemorate and bewail the Massacre, as they still affect to call it of the 5th of March. I am informed the Orator in the most express terms has declared that the Parliament has no power of Legislation over the Colonies. The Town have voted him thanks and desired him to print his harangue.

Hutchinson thought Lovell's harangue would convince Parliament to take away the town's power to host these incendiary gatherings.

Parliament did not act, however, and the next year's commemoration was even larger. By the time town moderator John Hancock and the orator, Dr. Benjamin Church, arrived at Old South, the building was so packed that the two had to climb through a window. Church declared that mere words "can scarcely paint the horrid scene. Defenceless, prostrate, bleeding countrymen,—the piercing, agonizing groans,—the mingled moan of weeping relatives and friends—,these best can speak, to rouse the luke-warm into noble zeal,—to fire the zealous into manly rage against the foul oppression of quartering troops in populous cities in times of peace!" Church praised the soldiers' acquittal, saying that Bostonians did not seek revenge, but "with haughty scorn we refused to become their executioners, and nobly gave them to the wrath of Heaven."

That evening on King Street, Mrs. Mary Clapham illuminated her windows next to the Exchange Tavern, featuring a long poem about the nature of revenge:

Ask not where Preston or his butchers are!
But ask, who brought these bloody villains here?

The town had not sought revenge on Preston, instead focusing its wrath on the political powers who had ordered the soldiers to Boston.

A broadside published that day, "A Monumental Inscription on the Fifth of March," has a few lines on the "Enlargement of Ebenezer Richardson." Beneath a woodcut rendition of the Revere engraving, the broadside calls on Americans to remember the HORRID MASSACRE that left five of their countrymen "wallowing in their Gore." Worse than the fact that only two of the soldiers were convicted—of manslaughter—and the others acquitted "by a Jury, of whom I shall say NOTHING!" was the fact that Ebenezer Richardson, convicted in April 1770, as of March 1772 still "Remains UNHANGED!!!"

The broadside blamed "weak and wicked monarchs, Tyrannical Ministers, Abandoned Governors, Their Underlings and Hirelings," and the "artful, designing Wretches" who wished to "ENSLAVE THIS People." An attached poem warned that though Richardson awaited his pardon from the King, "Heaven's laws will stand when KINGS shall die," and

Tho' Cushing's eas'd you from the prison gate
The [Trow] Bridge of Tories, it has borne you o'er
Yet you e'er long may meet with HELL's dark shore.

Two days earlier, on March 3, Hutchinson (the "Abandoned Governor") had received instructions to pardon Richardson. Hutchinson waited a week, and while the town leaders and radicals were busy with the town meeting, had Richardson brought into court, given his pardon, and quickly spirited out of town on a ferry. "The Rabble heard of it," Peter Oliver wrote, "and pursued him to execute their own Law upon him, but he happily escaped." Richardson never returned to Boston.

John Adams was invited to deliver the March 1773 oration. He was struck by the irony of the invitation, and declined it, as so many "irresistible Syllogisms rushed into my mind" that he did not know which to mention first. Most important was "the Reason that had hitherto actuated the Town" not to invite him, "the Part I took in the Tryal of the Soldiers." Adams knew that the commemorative oration "was quite compatible with the Verdict of the Jury," and "even with the absolute Innocence of the Soldiers." It was British colonial policy, not the soldiers sent to enforce it, that provoked the violence. While he could have made this point in an oration, he would "only expose myself to the Lash of ignorant and malicious tongues on both Sides of the Question. Besides that I was too old to make Declamations."

Instead of Adams, the town invited Dr. Joseph Warren, though Hutchinson wrote dismissively that Warren "gained no great applause for his oratorical abilities." But the Roxbury physician's "fervor, which is the most essential part of such compositions" had a great effect on the crowd at Old South. Warren focused squarely on Parliament's power to legislate for the colonies. He said that it had never occurred to "our ancestors, that, after so many dangers in this then desolate wilderness, their hard-earned property should be at the disposal of the British Parliament," and that when Parliament realized it could not persuade them through reason and argument to forfeit their property, "it seemed necessary that one act of oppression should be enforced by another," and so sent a "standing army ... among us in a time of peace" to enforce laws that violated the constitution.

Mrs. Clapham's balcony this year displayed a lantern show titled "The Fatal Effects of a Standing Army in a Free City." On the west end was the mourning figure of America looking down to the crowd on King Street, saying, "Behold my Sons!" On the east side a panel showed a monument inscribed with the victims' names. At quarter past nine the lanterns were extinguished, and the town church bells began to toll.

That night John Adams reflected in his diary on the Boston Massacre. "I have reason to remember that fateful night," he wrote. In hindsight, he thought his defense of Preston and the soldiers was "one of the most gallant, generous, manly, and disinterested Actions of my whole Life," and "one of the best pieces of Service I ever rendered my Country." According to the evidence, "the Verdict of the Jury was exactly right," and a "Judgment of Death against those Soldiers would have been as foul a Stain upon this Country as the Executions of the Quakers and Witches, anciently."

This would be the last relatively peaceful observance of the anniversary of the massacre. When Warren spoke on March 5, 1773, the uneasy peace that had existed since the troops went to Castle Island was beginning to unravel. Governor Hutchinson had opened the Assembly two months earlier, on January 5, with a long speech explaining the respective roles of the Massachusetts Assembly and the Parliament. He insisted that if Parliament did not have the power to govern Massachusetts, then Massachusetts was not part of the British Empire, but independent. He thought that a clear and compelling explanation would be enough to embolden those of his listeners whose loyalty to the Empire was sincere, and to expose those whose professions of loyalty were convenient masks of treason. But his strategy failed. The assembly, given the choice between submitting to the will of Parliament and being independent, took no time to decide the question Hutchinson had raised. Did Parliament govern Massachusetts, or did the people of Massachusetts govern themselves?

If Hutchinson believed that he, as the representative of the British crown, had power over the assembly, then the assembly would ask the Crown to replace Hutchinson with a governor more in line with the assembly's view of the province's constititution. Now John Adams, who had pilloried Crispus Attucks as the leader of a mob in 1770, attacked Hutchinson in the voice of Attucks. He drafted a newspaper blurb, never published, in July 1773, in the form of a "letter" from Attucks to Thomas Hutchinson. "You will hear from Us with Astonishment," Adams had his fictional Attucks write, on behalf of all the massacre victims. "You ought to hear from Us with Horror," for Hutchinson was "chargeable before God and Man, with our Blood." The soldiers had been "but passive Instruments" of Hutchinson's diabolical malevolence. The soldiers had no more independent moral judgment than did the "leaden Pellets" they fired, while Hutchinson was their master. He had "acted coolly, deliberately, and with all that premeditated Malice, not against Us in Particular,but against the People in general"—and in the eyes of the law this "is an ingredient in the Composition of Murder."While Thomas Hutchinson would never be tried for bringing on the massacre, Attucks warned him, "You will hear further from Us hereafter."

Finally, after a year of escalating disgust with British rule, the passage of the Tea Act in 1773 brought things to a boiling point. Bostonians learned they would have to buy tea only from English ships, which would be consigned only to particular merchants, and pay a tax on the tea. When the tea ships arrived at the end of 1773, the Sons of Liberty responded by throwing the tea into the harbor. This was the greatest uprising since the night of March 5, 1770, but unlike that horrible night, the so-called Boston Tea Party was a nonviolent demonstration. Parliament now had had enough, and in early 1774 suspended the government of Massachusetts, closed the port of Boston, and in May replaced Hutchinson with General Thomas Gage, the commander of Britain's military forces in North America.

John Hancock gave the annual March 5 oration in 1774, and he spoke eloquently of the loss of public virtue brought on by the arrival of the British troops. One of the wealthiest men in the province, Hancock told the audience, "Despise the glare of wealth. The people who pay greater respect to a wealthy villain than to an honest, upright man in poverty, almost deserve to be enslaved." That night, Mrs. Clapham's illuminations showed images of Governor Hutchinson and Judge Peter Oliver, with a poem:

Ye traitors! Is there not some chosen curse—
Some hidden thunder in the stores of heaven,

Red with uncommon wrath, to blast the men
Who owe their greatness to their country's ruin?

By the year's end, General Gage had brought the British military back to Boston, and by the early months of 1775 the town was firmly in the army's grip. When Joseph Warren arrived at Old South to deliver the annual March 5 oration in 1775, he found the hall packed not only with Bostonians, but also with British officers and soldiers. The Royal Welch Fusiliers packed the pulpit stairs and even the pulpit, hoping to intimidate Warren or force the agitated civilians to attack them. But Warren did not press his way through the crowd. Instead, clad in his orator's toga, he climbed through the window behind the pulpit, a dramatic entrance that shifted attention from the British officers to the Roxbury doctor. As in 1770, he said, "Our streets are again filled with armed men; our harbor crowded with ships of war. But these cannot intimidate us; our liberty must be preserved, it is far dearer than life."

As he spoke, one of the officers seated on the pulpit stairs tried to distract Warren by holding up a handful of bullets. Without pausing in his passionate oration, Warren dropped a handkerchief over the officer's hand. Within a few weeks, war began at the towns of Lexington and Concord; in June Warren himself died at Bunker Hill.

With the British army occupying Boston in 1776, Mary Clapham did not have her annual lantern show. Now her only tenants were British officers, one of whom, according to tradition, eloped with one of Mrs. Clapham's daughters. The annual massacre commemoration was held in Watertown, with Peter Thacher's oration featuring a long discourse on Joseph Warren's death in battle the previous June. The British forces in Boston were preoccupied in March 1776 with matters other than Thacher's speech.

Even though the British occupied Boston, the surrounding countryside was in the hands of rebel forces, now led by George Washington of Virginia. Boston bookseller Henry Knox (the same Knox who had warned sentry Hugh White that if he fired, he would die for it), had brought the cannon to Washington from Fort Ticonderoga. The guns were placed on the Dorchester Heights (now in South Boston) on the night of March 4.

General William Howe, the chief British strategist, ordered the first assault on Nook Hill on the morning of March 5. Washington demanded to know if his troops would allow the British to take their position on "the fifth of March!" The Bostonians would not allow this, and neither would Mother Nature, as a sudden snow squall dispersed Howe's attack.

Two weeks later, with Dorchester Neck firmly under Washington's control, and the cannon perched on its heights threatening their ships and fortifications, the British evacuated Boston. It was the first victory in the American Revolution.

The British had so damaged the Old South Meeting House during the occupation (by using it as a riding school) that in 1777 and after the town held the annual March 5 orations in the Old Brick Meeting House. On March 5, 1783, as the long war was ending, Dr. Thomas Welsh delivered the oration: "At length, independence is ours!" he announced. "Heaven commands! . . . All nations meet, and beat their swords into ploughshares and their spears into pruning-hooks, and resolve to learn war no more. Henceforth shall the American wilderness blossom as the rose, and every man shall sit under his fig-tree, and none shall make him afraid."

That day in Faneuil Hall, the town meeting voted to shift the annual commemoration from March 5, which recalled the Boston Massacre, to July 4, celebrating national independence. The men and women who remembered the Fifth of March were dying; new generations, with other concerns, problems, and ambitions, were taking their place. July 4, celebrating the possibilities of American society, rather than March 5, became the patriotic day. And so the massacre and other events of the Revolutionary struggle receded from living memory.

But in the 1850s the massacre came back into Boston's consciousness. William Cooper Nell, a black scholar intent on showing that African Americans were part of American history, wrote a pamphlet on the services of black patriots in the American Revolution. He expanded this into a book, *Colored Patriots of the American Revolution*, published in 1855. Both pamphlet and book began by discussing the Boston Massacre, calling out the notable fact that Crispus Attucks had been the first to die in the revolutionary cause.

Nell was writing at a time when the institution of slavery threatened to spread. With the Fugitive Slave Law of 1850, slaveowners had tightened the bonds of slavery across the country, and black men and women, even in free Boston, could be seized as runaway property. Nell's book affirmed that black men had fought for the cause of liberty, fighting in every major battle of the Revolutionary war. To remind white Americans of the black commitment to their liberty, Nell and a group of African Americans petitioned the state legislature in 1851 to build a monument to Crispus Attucks. The state refused.

On March 6, 1857, the U.S. Supreme Court issued its infamous Dred Scott decision, saying that at the time of the American Revolution, a "black man had no rights which a white man was bound to respect." Boston's black community was outraged. The following year, instead of holding a day of mourning on March 6, the anniversary of the Dred Scott decision, as other communities did, Boston's African Americans held the first annual Crispus Attucks Day rally at Faneuil Hall—on March 5. It was a vivid reminder that eighty-eight years earlier, when, according to the U.S. Supreme Court, a "black man had no rights which a white man was bound to respect," the town of Boston had placed Crispus Attucks's body in Faneuil Hall, thousands of Bostonians had marched in his funeral procession, and a British officer and eight soldiers were tried for his murder.

A teapot that Attucks owned went on display at Faneuil Hall, treated as a sacred relic. Also displayed were the flag John Hancock had given to George Middleton, commander of a black Revolutionary war regiment, the "Bucks of America"; and a copy of Emmanuel Leutze's painting *Washington Crossing the Delaware*, which depicts a black sailor, Prince Whipple, pulling an oar. A new lithograph of the massacre itself showed Crispus Attucks standing as the central figure in the crowd, boldly attacking the British soldiers. The Revolutionary-era patriots had shown Attucks and the others as innocent victims; now Attucks was depicted as the bold instigator he had been. Crispus Attucks Day became an annual event during the Civil War and for the years immediately after. On March 5, 1870, the centennial of the massacre, Boston's abolitionist paper *Commonwealth* noted that "American history could never have been perfected without a Negro as a conspicuous participant." The editor wrote that "Attucks had a share in the common feeling of the community, and the dream of freedom was as sweet to him as to his white associates."

The abolitionist movement put Crispus Attucks at the center of this 1856 lithograph of the massacre. *(Courtesy of the Bostonian Society)*

The Civil War revival of Crispus Attucks and the other victims of the Massacre had as its purpose the incorporation of black citizens into the nation's political fabric. As Boston began to build monuments to the Civil War, some wondered why, aside from the Bunker Hill Monument, Boston had no markers of the Revolution. In fact, an expanding Boston was quickly destroying the remaining Revolutionary-era buildings: John Hancock's house was demolished in 1863; Old South Meeting House was threatened with destruction by fire in 1872, and by its own church members (who had built an elegant new church in the Back Bay) a few years later. In 1881 the city of Boston planned to demolish the Old State House to clear the land for commercial development. This provoked an outcry from some Bostonians who wanted to save these historic buildings.

Private individuals committed to preserving history saved both Old South Meeting House and the Old State House. The Bostonian Society formed in 1881 to preserve the Old State House and to document Boston's history, which was quickly changing. The area around King Street (which became State Street after the Revolution) had changed

The Boston Massacre monument on Boston Common (Courtesy of the Bostonian Society)

radically since March of 1870. Only the Old State House remained, and it was quickly being surrounded by skyscrapers. (Boston's first skyscraper, the Ames Building, stood across the street.) Bostonian Society president Curtis Guild suggested in 1886 that the city place a monument on the massacre site. William Cooper Nell and a group of African Americans had suggested this same thing, and been turned down, thirty-five years earlier. But Guild was a leading white citizen (whose son would eventually be elected governor of Massachusetts), and he found the city more agreeable. In 1887 the city placed a marker on State Street: a circle of granite stones with thirteen spokes radiating out from the supposed spot (it was somewhat wide of the mark) "where the blood dripped from the wound of Attucks when he fell."

With the memorial in place, abolitionist leader Lewis Hayden and a group of African Americans proposed a marker for the victims' common, unmarked grave. The site would have been forgotten had the city not put an iron fence around the Granary Burying Ground in 1840. Excavations to install the fence had disturbed a northeast corner gravesite, where six skeletons, killed apparently by gunshots, lay together. These, it was conjectured, were the victims of the massacre and Christopher Seider, and now Hayden enlisted the support of civic leaders as well as Boston's black and abolitionist communities to give them a suitable monument. William Gaston, Hugh O'Brien, and Patrick Collins, all of whom had served or would serve as mayor, and Benjamin F. Butler, George D. Robinson, and N. P. Banks, former and future governors, joined Hayden and poet John Boyle O'Reilly, editor of the Catholic newspaper the *Boston Pilot*, in circulating a petition to mark the grave of the massacre victims.

The Massachusetts Legislature in May 1887 appropriated ten thousand dollars to build a "suitable memorial or monument" and to place headstones on the victims' graves. The city of Boston appropriated two thousand dollars to build a base for the monument. But now some of the supporters of marking the graves—notably the Massachusetts Historical Society and the New England Historic Genealogical Society—backed away, protesting against building an additional monument for the victims.

The Massachusetts Historical Society protested to the governor, hoping he would veto the legislature's proposal. Lawyer Charles Deane thought that Judge Trowbridge's charge to the jury was the best history of the event, and lamented that "the martyr's crown is placed upon the brow of the vulgar ruffian." Abner C. Goodell of the New England Historic Genealogical Society protested that the legislature had gone beyond the petition's intention in its plan to build a separate monument. He saw a big difference between "commemorating the first instance of bloodshed in Boston by British soldiers," an event that led to independence, and "applauding the unlawful action of rioters." Although the massacre itself prompted the removal of British troops, Goodell did not think "the mob in King Street" had "high motives and aspirations" and thus he believed they did not deserve to be memorialized for their individual actions. Bostonians would not condone mobs in 1887, Goodell argued, and thus they should not build monuments to a mob of 1770; "monuments of stone will not avail to perpetuate an error of history."

Despite these arguments, Governor Oliver Ames—as a former bank and railroad president, no friend to lawless mobs—chose a site on Boston Common. On November 14, 1888, official representatives of the Commonwealth and the City dedicated the monument, a twenty-five foot granite pillar with thirteen stars circling the top. Below the stars are the names of the five victims: Crispus Attucks, Samuel Maverick, James Caldwell, Samuel Gray, and Patrick Carr.

Both the pillar, and the seven-foot statue of Free America crushing a crown with her right foot, stand on a granite base. Inset into the base, at eye level, is a bas-relief of the Paul Revere/Henry Pelham scene of the massacre. Lying lifeless in the foreground is the body of Crispus Attucks, and a musket is being fired from the Custom House window. Two quotations are inscribed on the bas-relief. One is from Daniel Webster, the great nineteenth-century exponent of law and order: "From that moment we may date the severance of the British Empire." The other, ironically but appropriately, is from John Adams: "On that night the foundation of American Independence was laid."

The Crispus Attucks Lodge of the Knights of Pythias joined a procession of military bands and marchers at the corner of Beacon and Charles streets and proceeded to the State House, where Governor Oliver Ames joined them for the march to the monument. After the Germania band played "America," Reverend Eli Smith offered a prayer invoking the Civil War as well as the Revolution, and the "oppressed race" that was central to both. He thanked God "that the first blood of the revolutionary conflict was shed by a black man, a representative of the race with whom so many of us here are identified." From the Common, the procession marched up Tremont Street, passing the victims' graves, down Court Street, passing by what was now Washington Street, where in the last moments of his life Crispus Attucks had led a party of twenty-five sailors to attack the British Main Guard, stepping over the spot where he had died; then up Merchants Row to Faneuil Hall.

One hundred eighteen years earlier, Attucks's body had been carried from Faneuil Hall, followed by more people than had ever before gathered in North America. The delegation entering the hall in November 1888 was smaller but equally diverse. It included black abolitionist Lewis Hayden, Governor Ames, Mayor Hugh O'Brien, Robert Treat Paine, Jr., a descendant of the prosecutor, Pierre B. S. Pinchback, the first African American elected to the United States Senate, Curtis Guild of the Bostonian Society, and other dignitaries and ordinary citizens.

The committee had invited the great abolitionist orator Frederick Douglass to deliver the address, but Douglass, then seventy years old, living in the District of Columbia, regretfully declined, writing that he would have been honored to join Massachusetts in taking the lead "in honoring the memory of patriots and heroes, of whatever race and color," and that he did not doubt that one day "the colored man will have the same measure of justice accorded him by others that Massachusetts now accords to Crispus Attucks, the hero of the State-street massacre in 1770."

While much of the attention was on Attucks, the focus of the ceremony was broader. The principal poet was John Boyle O'Reilly, who wrote these words for the occasion:

Where shall we seek for a hero, and where shall we find a story?
Our laurels are wreathed for conquest, our songs for completed glory;
But we honor a shrine unfinished, a column uncapped with pride,
If we sing the deed that was sown like seed when Crispus Attucks died.

"Call it riot or revolution, or mob or crowd as you may, / Such deaths have been seed of nations," the poem continued. While the "lackeys" regarded Attucks and the others as "lawless hind," they were "martyrs to Paul Revere." For O'Reilly, Attucks embodied all oppressed people, and the lesson Attucks taught "in the old heroic way" was that "God made mankind to be one in blood, as one in spirit and light."

Harvard history professor John Fiske delivered the principal address. Fiske was a rather conservative historian, and though he did not name anyone, he spoke of the scholars who "belittled or aspersed" the motives of Attucks and the others in King Street on March 5. He spoke of the clamoring and protesting of Bostonians trying to get the troops out of town, and noted that Attucks, Gray, Caldwell, Maverick, and Carr had by their deaths "effected in a moment what seventeen months of petition and discussion had failed to accomplish." Thanks to these men, Fiske said, Bostonians would no longer be intimidated by British soldiers; now the soldiers would be wary of Bostonians. Fiske noted that many historians were focusing on the "maligned and misunderstood" Tories (supporters of the Crown), and in doing so had "swung around into the Tory view of the events" in a way that would " make glorious old Samuel Adams turn in his grave."

But the building of the monument insured that Samuel Adams's view of the event would ultimately prevail, and the victims' story would still inspire. Teenager Malcolm Little arrived from the Midwest in 1940 to live with an aunt in Roxbury. Venturing out of the black community, he explored Boston's landmarks, and later, after he had become Malcolm X, he recalled: "One statue in the Boston Commons astonished me: a Negro named Crispus Attucks, who had been the first man to fall in the Boston Massacre. I had never known anything like that."

The marking of the street in 1887, and the building of a monument in 1888, fixed the Boston Massacre as a historical event. It became an indelible part of the historical narrative of the Revolution, though still a paradoxical one. The victims were not prominent men of the day; they were unknowns, and their motives were obscure. The soldiers who killed them were defended by Josiah Quincy and John Adams, two men who were neither unknown nor obscure, and who were firmly on the side of the soldiers' victims. Attucks, Gray, Maverick, Caldwell, or Carr may not have intended to start a revolution, but with their deaths they did so.

BIBLIOGRAPHY

HILLER B. ZOBEL'S *The Boston Massacre* (New York: W.W. Norton & Company, Inc., 1970) is the standard and authoritative source on the Massacre and the events leading up to it. Judge Zobel and L. Kinvin Wroth's *The Legal Papers of John Adams* (Cambridge: The Belknap Press of Harvard University, 1965) contains transcripts of the trials and superb notes. I thank Judge Zobel for these monumental works of scholarship, and for his careful reading of this manuscript.

The town of Boston's report, and transcripts of the trials, can also be found in Frederick Kidder's *History of the Boston Massacre, Consisting of the Narrative of the Town, the Trial of the Soldiers, and a Historical Introduction* (originally published 1870; reissued Delran, New Jersey: Classics of Liberty Library, 2001).

Pauline Maier's *From Resistance to Revolution: Colonial Radicals and the Development of American Opposition to Britain, 1765-1776* (New York: Alfred A. Knopf, 1972) remains indispensable on the tumultuous political climate of 1770, and connections between the ideas of British radicals and the Sons of Liberty.

In addition, the manuscript and 18th-century document collections at the Massachusetts State Archives, the Massachusetts Historical Society, and the Bostonian Society have been invaluable. Special thanks to Michael Comeau of the Massachusetts Archives, Peter Drummey of the Massachusetts Historical Society, and Christopher Carden of the Bostonian Society for their guidance in these collections.

Above all, thanks to my friend and colleague Professor Joseph McEttrick of the Suffolk University Law School, whose re-enactment of the Wemms trial at Faneuil Hall in May of 2000 awakened my own interest in the Massacre and its aftermath.

INDEX

Note: Page references given in **bold** indicate illustrations or their captions

CPSIA information can be obtained at www.ICGtesting.com
Printed in the USA
LVOW10s1619081014

407868LV00002B/329/P